The Marks
of Scripture

The Marks
of Scripture

Rethinking the Nature of the Bible

Daniel Castelo and Robert W. Wall

Baker Academic

a division of Baker Publishing Group
Grand Rapids, Michigan

Published by Baker Academic
a division of Baker Publishing Group
PO Box 6287, Grand Rapids, MI 49516-6287
www.bakeracademic.com

Printed in the United States of America

Library of Congress Cataloging-in-Publication Data
Names: Castelo, Daniel, 1978– author. | Wall, Robert W., author.
Title: The marks of Scripture : rethinking the nature of the Bible / Daniel Castelo and
    Robert W. Wall.
Description: Grand Rapids, MI : Baker Academic, a division of Baker Publishing
    Group, [2019] | Includes bibliographical references and indexes.
Identifiers: LCCN 2018023227 | ISBN 9780801049552 (paper : alk. paper)
Subjects: LCSH: Bible—Theology. | Nicene Creed. | Church—Marks.
Classification: LCC BS543 .C28 2018 | DDC 220.1—dc23
LC record available at https://lccn.loc.gov/2018023227

ISBN 978-1-5409-6150-1 (casebound)

19 20 21 22 23 24 25   7 6 5 4 3 2 1

In memoriam
John Webster
(1955–2016)

Contents

Preface

This book is the product of both a friendship and a shared passion. Our friendship has been forged over a decade at our institutional home, Seattle Pacific University and Seminary. During this time we have had many conversations about a host of things. We truly enjoy one another's company. Our friendship is a gift from God that we cherish very much. We also share a number of passions. One of those shared passions is a deep love for Scripture. Our passion for and confidence in Scripture is grounded in a shared affirmation of its vast potential as a sanctifying auxiliary of God's Spirit in transforming the church's worship, instruction, mission, and devotional life in fresh and powerful ways. We practice Scripture because we have seen the Spirit use it to convict, shape, and change people's lives into conformity to our Lord. We hope this passion is evident in the classroom when we teach our students, nonbelievers and believers alike, and also in our published work. We are intellectually hospitable to engage in conversations with any others over matters of common concern; however, we gladly come to that conference table with firm convictions about the Bible's authority and its continuing relevance for our day. We hope this book clarifies those convictions going forward.

This book is also a response to a shared concern about the nature of theological discourse and the curricula that instantiate it in many divinity schools. Simply put, theologians and biblical scholars have compartmentalized their investigations and conversations about the core beliefs and practices of the Christian faith they share. Scripture is taught and its meaning reconstructed within the ancient social worlds that come with particular texts. Bible faculty only rarely vest their study of these texts with the dogmatic insight of their theologian colleagues. Although this interaction has happily begun within the guilds of biblical scholarship (e.g., the Society of Biblical Literature, the Studiorum Novi Testamenti Societas, the Institute for Biblical Research), it has yet to trickle down to the seminary classroom, where courses in "theological interpretation" are still uncommon, and team-taught courses of theologians and biblical scholars even less so. We find the same is true of professional theologians whose instruction on the church's theological goods is often more fluent in contemporary sociological or anthropological models than in biblical studies. We hope, then, this book will be read not so much as an indictment of the "Christ-Scripture" or "incarnational analogy" but principally as an example of the kind of discourse we long for in theological education today: a theologian and a biblical scholar engaged in a mutually glossing conversation over a common theme by utilizing methods and contributions from each discipline to construct a whole greater than the sum of its two parts.

As for those in our classrooms, we often present ourselves as teachers and doctors of and for the church, but sometimes even our Christian students are not as passionate as we are about Scripture. Many hold it in high regard but confess their trust as a routine shibboleth or theological abstraction; they do not know how to talk about the importance they willingly grant Scripture. Ironically, they have learned from others how to affirm their Bible beliefs but not how to articulate why they trust Scripture without budge or blush. Others are dismayed by the way some Christians deny or shortchange what is plainly in the text so as to conform Scripture to fit some predetermined understanding. We find that the primary reason for this situation is a lack of imagination in how congregations teach their membership, including our Christian students, how to think and talk about the Scripture they affirm as a revelatory word. We hope our book sparks an imaginative conversation for our students and their teachers about a new way to envision Scripture's nature and enduring authority.

In terms of audience, we seek a broad readership that reflects the whole church. We are both faculty members and so naturally had students and their teachers in mind when we wrote this book. Even though not technically academic, it is scholarly enough for use in the academy. Put another way, we did not necessarily write this text for other scholars: the work is not heavily footnoted, and specific details or alternatives were sometimes not pursued for the sake of brevity. We wrote intuitively and experimentally—off the cuff, if you will—so as not to overburden the text with documentation and to preserve some of the energy and vitality with which we come to writing this particular book. There are some loose ends here and there, we know. And yet, we are inclined to author pieces this way occasionally (in addition to our more technical writings) for the sake of the church. Our shared conviction that we are doctors of and for the church sometimes puts us at odds with the academy and sometimes puts us at odds with the church. We believe that the wide chasm between these two constituencies is all too often an intellectual and formational mistake. This work is an extension of our desire to see that gap bridged.

One final note to clarify terminology and style: We take a broad approach to our use of "the church." We are not bound to use this term along rigid, confessional lines. We are Methodists with Pentecostal roots. We are inclined to join Irenaeus and say that where the church is, there is the Spirit of God, and vice versa (*Against Heresies* 3.24.1). And, we would add, the Spirit of God is evident where people are attentive to the word of God and seek to form loving relationships with God and neighbor. When speaking of "Scripture" we have in mind the two-Testament canon of sacred texts that a faithful people affirm as authoritative and so practice in their worship, instruction, mission, and personal devotions for holy ends. As for the style of this book, we wanted to preserve our distinct voices amid our shared convictions. Therefore, in the chapters devoted to the marks, we begin and conclude with general remarks, but within the chapters themselves are sections distinctly authored by each of us. As for the other chapters, we attempted to maintain a unity of style and thus revised them extensively. Throughout, we liberally use plural first-person pronouns, a demonstration of the extent of our shared visions.

The origins of this book lie in the sanctified imagination of Rob; this was originally his idea to pursue. Rob decided that the idea would be best developed as a collaboration between a Scripture scholar and a theologian, and so Daniel was brought along. We went on to coauthor "Scripture and the Church: A Précis for an Alternative Analogy," which serves as a precursor to this book. Since this article's publication, we have developed the analogy we seek to explore here in a variety of publications and settings, both academic and ecclesial. When appropriate, we have identified these explorations in footnotes, grateful to our colleagues and students for their feedback. The conversation continues, and we trust that the publication of this work moves the argument from a précis to a more substantial contribution.

We are thankful for the splendid editorial work of Baker Academic's Eric Salo, who worked hard editing this manuscript to make a dialogue between two like-minded colleagues from different theological disciplines more coherent and persuasive. We also thank Carla Wall for taking time out from a busy life to read through the galleys of our prospective book as an "ideal reader" to offer her suggestions for greater clarity and better arguments.

Finally, this book is the by-product of many conversations inspired and cultivated within a collegial community marked by its intellectual hospitality and genuine care for one another. In addition to our colleagues in the School of Theology at Seattle Pacific University, we acknowledge with thanksgiving Stephen Fowl of Loyola University of Maryland for his indispensable contributions to our way of thinking about a theology of Scripture and its theological interpretation.

Sadly, however, a recent development made the choice of dedication clear. Even though he is in the company of our Lord, we continue to be saddened by the loss represented in the passing of John Webster. As is quite obvious in these pages, we are influenced significantly by his work, especially his *Holy Scripture: A Dogmatic Sketch*. In many ways we were hoping to extend some of the arguments in that work with our present volume. When Daniel talked to Webster about this project some time ago, he was intrigued and supportive of the idea in its nascent form. His voice is missed, yet we are full of joy that his life had such an impact on so many, including ourselves. We are looking forward to the day when we will join him and the rest of the heavenly audience, proclaiming for all eternity the words of Isaiah 6:3:

> "Holy, holy, holy is the LORD of hosts; the whole earth is full of his glory."

Daniel Castelo and Robert W. Wall
Epiphany 2018
Seattle, Washington

1

The Ontology
and Teleology of Scripture

What is Scripture? What is its purpose? These are two key questions any thoughtful, earnest, and God-loving reader of the Bible should ask. And yet, rarely do Christians raise them in their reading and reflective practices. The first question can be said to be the ontological question: What is the nature of Scripture's essence and so its identity? The second question can be labeled teleological: What is the function of Scripture, and for what end do people read it? These are such basic questions that one simply assumes Christians intuitively have answers at their disposal. "The Bible is God's word and so truth," one could say, further adding, "and Christians read it in order to know God and God's truth." These claims, however, are largely tautologous; they simply affirm and reaffirm a commitment one has to Scripture's authority, but they do little to secure that authority within a wider paradigm. They suggest nothing in terms of different conceptions of truth, the character of God, or the general nature of interpretation overall. Rather than being deliberate answers to the ontological and teleological questions, these responses are deferrals that bypass the hard work of reflecting *about* Scripture.

1

Reflecting about Scripture must be undertaken by Christians in the sense that Scripture is not simply a text they read: it is also a theological category. When Christians speak of Scripture, appeal to it, or assume its authority, they do so in ways that are inherently theological; they implicitly recognize Scripture as *being* theologically significant, even though they may not consciously acknowledge the gesture. Perhaps this point was more obvious for previous generations who were inclined to call the Bible "Holy Writ," "the Holy Bible," or "the sacred Word." Calling this text "holy" can suggest that it operates in God's "economy of sanctification"—the ways and means by which a holy God shapes and transforms a community into a holy people. Whether it is recognized as such in the contemporary scene, Scripture is a category of theological consequence. It has a role to play in God's manifest work, and this role helps constitute both its identity and its function in the life of the faithful.

Remarkable about academic and popular approaches to Christian Scripture, however, is that something on occasion happens. Rather than thinking of Scripture as a theological category, many look to Scripture as a basis, source, or foundation for doing theology. The difference in this claim is slight but significant. Rather than being a theological category, Scripture is sometimes employed as a resource for theologizing. In this approach, Scripture provides the "source material" for doing theology, but Scripture is not considered outright as theological at its very core. This approach to Scripture is not altogether wrong, but it does present a number of challenges that cannot be easily overcome on their own. Some of these difficulties are highlighted by the following questions: If Scripture is not understood as a theological category, then how can it be categorized or classified? If Scripture is used strictly as a resource for theology, then what does that say about how theology is pursued and the kind of theology that will ensue from this casting? Do other ways of understanding Scripture exist, and if so, why is this first model often privileged? These questions are crucial, particularly since Christians generally, and Protestants particularly (given the way they cast their specific identity), have so much at stake with matters related to the Bible. No Christian will deny the importance of the Bible for Christian identity, but different proposals are available as to how to understand its authority. These differences matter because they reflect and determine various intellectual and spiritual sensibilities that are at work in interpreting and applying Scripture, and differences on these scores in turn will inevitably shape how one views the Christian life and the Christian God.

In what follows, we will begin a process of engaging Scripture as a theological category by considering it as canon and as a means of grace. In this way, Scripture will be cast as theologically consequential rather than instrumental, a topic of proper theological consideration rather than one that is passed over so as to rush to the pursuit of doing "real theology." We consider this work crucial as we begin this text; these understandings will inflect all that we subsequently say about the Bible.

As to the first term, "canon" has the advantage of being a theological category that prominently involves both anthropological and pneumatological dimensions. We argue that the same can be said for the term "Scripture," yet since the Bible is so significantly determined by many Christian constituencies, those points (the anthropological and pneumatological) may be harder to identify and promote, at least at the outset of a discussion. A focus on canon can show that this text is both historical and revelatory, human- and Spirit-generated, and this makes for a more nuanced treatment of the many features of Scripture as a theological phenomenon.

As to the second term, a "means of grace" suggests a different kind of tension: how God and humans are involved in spiritual formation and sanctification. Christians of all kinds read Scripture devotionally in order to foster growth and development in their spiritual journeys. In this, they are approaching Scripture as a means of grace. This kind of activity and practice associated with Scripture is theologically significant. It is academically noteworthy because any treatment of Scripture within the theological academy needs to account for the theological significance of this kind of appropriation; otherwise, we believe, the treatment will be theologically myopic.

With the terms "canon" and "means of grace," then, Scripture can be thought of in more ways than simply a deposit of theological building blocks. With these alternative castings, the ontology and teleology of the Bible may become clearer and more relevant, and if so, then its place within the life of the faithful can be richer and more explicitly and practically formative.

Scripture as Canon

Christians have always been people of the book. The special status granted to the church's Bible in Christian formation is sounded by the theological terms associated with it: "Scripture," "sacrament," "word," "canon," and so on. In particular, the idea that the Bible is a canon of sacred texts signifies it as a book that God's people should read and use in worship, catechesis, devotions, and discussions in order to learn about God and to form a manner of life and faith pleasing to God. The Bible is canon not because it is a singular rule that outperforms every other medium through which God's Spirit makes God known; rather, the Bible is canon precisely because of the indispensable, formative tasks it performs as an auxiliary of the Spirit in directing the church's life toward God. And because they are special in this particular way, the biblical texts selected, collected, and presented as canonical should be picked up, again and again, by every Christian congregation as required reading.

The language of "selection," "collection," and "presentation" suggests a dynamic that on occasion worries some Christians because it can seem too dependent on a historical process. Many wonder about and are even suspicious of this process. Given the conspiracy theories and hypothetical scenarios abounding in popular culture, people may puzzle over why certain books were included while others were not. But a more fundamental worry for many is highlighted via the following question: How can a book that is assumed to be theologically authoritative as the "word of God" be so enmeshed in a process that is very much driven by human judgments and factors, ones that are prone to bias, limits, and ignorance? Of course, this worry is not ancillary to a discussion about Scripture's authority, but on theological grounds, this process cannot be reduced simply to a historical, human dynamic. The postbiblical circumstances and social world that now frame the historian's discussion of the canonical process should be understood in theological terms if Scripture is agreed upon as being a theological category. While John Webster agrees that canonization is a process of "human decision-making," he also describes it in terms of the sanctifying participation of the Spirit, whose presence intends to extend the apostolic testimony of the historical Jesus into the future.[1] In this sense, the various phenomena that historians ascribe to canonization can also be understood as Spirit-led events that safeguard and textually establish the normative truth about Christ.

As an act of confession, the church recognizes that among its membership in ages past it came to decide which texts best performed a canonical role in its common life. But this act of confession was not based on the church's savviness or trustworthiness throughout this process; more basically, the church's confession on this score is that the Holy Spirit inspired these texts, drove these texts to communal prominence, and guided the church in its selection processes so that fitting texts were included for the task of shaping a holy community. Far from spontaneous or chaotic, the canonization process—from a text's initial composition to its eventual canonization as part of a canonical collection in the church's two-Testament Bible—is both providential and purposeful. No point of this historical process is arbitrary or accidental; it is from beginning to end a creaturely process superintended by God's sanctifying Spirit for holy ends in the global church's worship, catechesis, mission, and personal devotions.[2] Put another way, as human-generated as this process may look when viewed through one lens (i.e., a "canonization from below"), viewed through another lens it is very much a God-determined development (i.e., a "canonization from above"). Humans did not simply make choices. Rather, God-fearing saints made certain judgments within

---

1. See Webster, *Holy Scripture*, 23–24, 50–52.

2. In fact, the partnership between God's Spirit and the church's Scripture continues beyond the initial writing of the text, and extends to the various ongoing performances by a faithful community of practice. "Scripture's ontology is directly tied to its teleology" (Castelo, *Pneumatology*, 93). That is, Scripture is infused and substantiated by the Spirit-illuminating roles for the divine economy of sanctification that forge a "decisive and full-orbed Christian existence" (ibid., 94)—what Wesleyans call "full salvation." In this sense, we lay claim to a more functional and expansive notion of Scripture's authority. The church receives Scripture as God's word and as an auxiliary of the Spirit who is at work through sanctifying agents to form God's holy people as a public witness to God's victory in Christ. See ibid., 90–94 for a précis of our "pneumatology of Scripture."

a Spirit-drenched context, one in which the Spirit was involved at the beginning, during the process, and toward the end of a complex series of developments called "canonization."

The church's "canon-consciousness," then, is the graced (God-given) capacity to discern what substantively agrees with the apostolic testimony of Jesus from what does not. The church's act of discernment is not a magical performance. This recognition of a text's canonicity, if properly led by the Spirit, is necessarily honed in worship by prayer and in faithful use when teaching and training God's people.[3] Canonization is a process of and for the church in which God's Spirit is present, performing the role for which the Spirit was sent (see John 14–16). There is no need for a biblical canon if there is no church, and without a biblical canon the church would be spiritually impoverished. For this practical reason, we insist (to highlight one of our major commitments in this book) that the marks of a Spirit-led community, which is competent to produce and use a canon of Scripture, will necessarily be of a piece with the marks of that book it produces and uses. This is the essential circularity of the canonical process.

Canonization is a complex but crucial phenomenon for the current discussion because its careful construction can help shape how one answers the ontological and teleological matters sketched above. In terms of Scripture's essence, one has to reply in light of the developmental nature of canonization that Scripture is not simply a category but a running argument, one that requires an ongoing set of judgments. And at one level, these judgments are ecclesial in nature: the worshiping faithful came to use and recognize certain texts as "useful for teaching, for reproof, for correction, and for training in righteousness" (2 Tim. 3:16) for those in its fold.

The church's episcopacy made these judgments at a moment of history wrapped in its own social world and exigencies.[4] Most historical studies of what we are calling a "canonization from below" are framed by the reconstruction of a variety of threats, both internal and external, which occasioned an epistemic crisis—"What is

3. Webster, *Holy Scripture*, 58–67.
4. For a summary of this history, see Wall, "Canon."

truth?"—that incited the formation of a Christian Bible. Although we are convinced that the community's canon-consciousness, shaped by its use of Israel's scripture and apostolic writings from the beginning (see 1 John 1:1–2), would have made the formation of this book inevitable, we agree that the urgency of doing so was made more so by the contested reception of the apostolic tradition during the second century. There were a variety of Christianities, which required a stable textual boundary within which theological and ethical matters could be debated and resolved as a practical matter of the church's unity.[5]

The pivotal figure in Adolf von Harnack's programmatic narrative on these matters is Marcion (ca. 85–ca. 160), whom the Apologists considered a rival of the apostles (although a Pauline tradent[6]) but who is reputed to be the first teacher to design and use a Christian Bible for catechetical purposes. According to Harnack's narrative, Marcion objected to the prevailing version of apostolic Christianity and sought to purify it of its Jewish theology and Hellenistic ethics by establishing a canon of Pauline Letters as revelatory of Christ's genuine gospel. In response to Marcion, the Apologists proposed a canon of their own, which enfolded Marcion's Pauline collection into a Christian Bible including the writings of the Lord's original apostles that Marcion had rejected.[7] Most who follow this plotline suspect that Marcion's motive for producing a discrete Christian Bible was to secure his apostolicity (see chap. 6 below). But perhaps it is better to understand his Bible as incited by the same canon-consciousness and awareness of the same apostolic writings that later shaped Irenaeus's conception of a Christian Bible. The materials Marcion gathered, based on the broad experience of various Christian (predominantly Gentile) congregations—an early edition of Luke's Gospel and a ten-letter collection of Paul's canonical letters to form a Gospel-Letter canon—had already begun to eclipse Israel's scripture in the

---

5. This intramural battle over the theological grammar of an "orthodox" faith is reflected in the pages of the New Testament. Again, an element of canon-consciousness is this practical concern of turning to certain texts in order to figure out God's word when this is the very thing being debated.

6. A *tradent* is any believer who belongs to and is shaped by the theological grammar of a particular apostolic tradition.

7. The most succinct narrative of Harnack's contested reconstruction of Marcion's influence is found in his massive *History of Dogma*, 1:266–81.

Bible practices of the apostolic community. One need not name-call Marcion a "supersessionist" when most of the church had already come to depend more on Paul than on the Pentateuch for its theological instruction at this time. In fact, Irenaeus himself recognized that the real "problem" with Marcion's canon was not that it was anti-apostolic but that it was an exclusively Pauline "canon within the canon," concentrating normative truth claims on the received writings of a single apostolic tradition (including Luke's Gospel), to the exclusion of the writings of the Jerusalem pillars and the Septuagint. Sharply put, the problem with Marcion's canon was that it had an incomplete shape and size, which had the deleterious effect of shaping an incomplete and ineffective theology for the church's life.

We might gloss this general observation pneumatologically by what we are calling a "canonization from above." That is, the use of Marcion's Pauline canon (and, even today, certain Protestant groups follow it in practice!) quenches the Spirit's various uses of Scripture by limiting the range of its pluriform prophetic and apostolic witness of the incarnate Word. Put positively, if the Spirit takes the lead in the canonical process by first choosing those writings that the church then recognizes as "divinely inspired," the literary product produced by that process—that is, the church's *textus receptus* in its final canonical form—must be approached and appropriated as maximally effective for the Spirit's own illuminating, formative work within the church. However, without this entire canon in full play, the Spirit's use of Scripture as an auxiliary of its teaching ministry to mark out God's people as one, holy, catholic, and apostolic will be seriously subverted.[8]

8. This notion of the Spirit's use of Scripture was informed by what the church deemed as helpful in the task of inspiring believers and keeping them faithful to Jesus and the teachings and preaching of the apostles. Often, when people speak of the canonical process, criteria are appealed to that are of a historical (authorial origins, context, and so on) as well as theological (how well a book coheres to other established books and so forth) nature. From these gleanings, people stamp the process as a recognition of a text's "inspiration," with the appeal sometimes made to 2 Tim. 3:16 ("All scripture is inspired by God"). Missing from this allusion, however, is the second half of the verse ("and is useful for teaching, for reproof, for correction, and for training in righteousness"), which might in turn function as a gloss on what the term "inspiration" may involve and how a text comes to be recognized as "inspired" in the first place. In this sense, "Scripture" is a dynamic

On the basis of a belief in God's providential work, we can claim that the Spirit's sanctification of the canonical process orders it in a precise and purposeful way, which has produced a biblical canon for the ongoing community of faith that effectively serves the holy ends appointed and enabled by the Spirit's inspiring presence. We might think of this in the same way the evangelist summarizes the announcement of the historical Jesus, who arrives into his first-century Palestinian world when "the time is fulfilled" (Mark 1:15). His messianic life is not somehow less than historical. The Creator's providential partnership with earthly creatures directs and animates them as the *necessary property of their material existence* toward an eternal end of God's own making. In other words, Jesus's Jewishness, shaped by his first-century Roman Palestinian world, is of a piece with his messianic mission, and that mission is of a piece with God's gracious and kindhearted purposes for all creation.

Our response to those critics who continue to fix the theological and hermeneutical importance of canonization and its literary production in an ancient past follows this same line of argument. The Bible's composition and canonization, as thoroughly creaturely activities, took place under the Spirit's direction in the fullness of time for the Spirit's use until kingdom come (when Scripture is no longer needed) as an auxiliary of the Spirit's illumination of God's purposes already realized through the risen One. Today's worshiping faithful should own the warrants and implications of such judgments, not because ancient others have deemed it so, but because their past judgments register God's design, reaffirmed time and again as effective from generation to generation of the church catholic whenever and wherever biblical texts are practiced and performed in congregational worship, catechesis, and mission. In this sense, Scripture is the church's book; its legal address is the church (the ontological dimension). Additionally, in this sense, Scripture was purposefully shaped and ordered to form the church's covenant-keeping communion with the living God for heaven's sake (the teleological dimension).

---

process, a dynamism shaped during the canonical process by historical and theological factors and by a formational impress as well.

Scripture as a Means of Grace

We are also inclined to think of Scripture as a means of grace. We are aware that this phrase can be off-putting for those who are not used to employing it. In our case, as Methodists, we use the language in a very specific way, drawing on an Anglican heritage that was embodied in the ministry and thought of John Wesley.

Wesley himself recognized that this language was potentially misleading. In a sermon by the same name, he offered this general definition: "By 'means of grace' I understand outward signs, words, or actions ordained of God, and appointed for this end—to be the *ordinary* channels whereby he might convey to men preventing, justifying, or sanctifying grace." Wesley says he uses the phrase because he knows none better, in that it was employed in the Church of England's delineation of sacraments. He notes, "In particular [the phrase is used] by our own church, which directs us to bless God both for the 'means of grace and hope of glory'; and teaches us that a sacrament is 'an outward sign of an inward *grace*, and a *means* whereby we receive the same.'"[9]

If Scripture is a means of grace in the sense noted above, what that rendering achieves is to place Scripture in the company of both spiritual disciplines and sacraments. Wesley continues, "The chief of these means are prayer, whether in secret or with the great congregation; searching the Scriptures (which implies reading, hearing, and meditating thereon) and receiving the Lord's Supper, eating bread and drinking wine in remembrance of him." He continues, "These we believe to be ordained of God as the ordinary channels of conveying his grace to the souls of men."[10] This collective casting is quite generative, for it suggests that a similar logic may be at work in each of the three "means" mentioned: prayer is akin to reading the Scriptures, and both are akin to partaking of the Lord's Supper. Within the triad, how one is understood has the potential to be relatable to how the other two are. Therefore, reading Scripture can be understood similarly to praying and to partaking of the sacrament of Communion. Reading Scripture, then, can and ought to be understood to some degree in terms of spiritual disciplines and sacraments.

9. Wesley, "Means of Grace," 381, including additional citations.
10. Wesley, "Means of Grace," 381.

Of course, in all three a formalism could emerge in which, despite "having a form of godliness," one ends up "denying the power thereof" (2 Tim. 3:5 KJV). Perhaps this would be the running reservation by many with the language of "means," but it should be refuted from the onset: The means of grace cannot be understood to be calculated means for achieving predetermined ends, all in a process that is accomplished primarily by human striving. Wesley is very well aware of the point. If these activities do not attend to the end of religion—that is, if they do not lead to the knowledge and love of God—they have no value before God's eyes; in fact, at such a point, they would be an abomination to God.[11] Therefore Wesley attends to the means of grace very much in terms of the way they are utilized. The modality of their use is crucial: How, in what manner, and to what end are they employed?

For Wesley, a doxological modality, one of worship, is primary here. Praying, reading Scripture, and partaking of the Lord's Supper are first and foremost worshipful activities. Christians undertake them to worship the living God and to commune with this God. Wesley straightforwardly remarks, "We know that there is no inherent power in the words that are spoken in prayer, in the letter of Scripture read, the sound thereof heard, or the bread and wine received in the Lord's Supper; but that it is God alone who is the giver of every good gift, the author of all grace."[12] In casting the means as doxological, Wesley places God front and center in their efficaciousness.

The theo-logic[13] of the means of grace is ascetical in a certain sense. That is to say, their inner workings involve both active and passive dimensions. The dynamic can be said to work in the following way: God's salvation is a graciously given gift, which is in turn received by faith via active forms of waiting. These active forms of waiting are otherwise known as "the means of grace."[14] In this, Wesley is trying to avoid many different extremes.[15] For one, we are not

11. Wesley, "Means of Grace," 381.
12. Wesley, "Means of Grace," 382.
13. We use the term "theo-logic" to show that theological discernment ("theo-") is a rational, logical process ("-logic").
14. Wesley, "Means of Grace," 383.
15. Wesley addresses many of the reservations in "Means of Grace," 390–93.

the meritorious cause of salvation; we cannot earn or accomplish our salvation because only one can save—namely, Christ. Therefore, we should not look to the practice of the means of grace as somehow achieving or guaranteeing anything on our behalf simply by our practice of them. And yet to press another point, we are not to sit idly by, waiting for God to appear in our midst, for that would lead to the heresy of quietism, which wrongfully locates the context of knowing God exclusively in privatized experiences we passively "feel." Contrary to this, Wesley believed that knowing God involves all that God has graciously provided the church to sustain, uphold, and transform it into God's likeness. Included in this heritage we are bequeathed as Christ-followers is Holy Writ. As Hal Knight declares of the Wesleyan view, "The identity of God can only be known by faith through participation in those means of grace which convey identity, such as scripture and the eucharist."[16]

When Wesley elaborates Scripture as a means of grace, he goes on to extensively engage the Timothy correspondence, which is significant for us in this work. The admonition of Paul to Timothy that Scripture can make him "wise unto salvation" (2 Tim. 3:15 KJV) applies to us today as well. And Wesley does not simply stop with the notion that Scripture is inspired but goes on to affirm (as we have been emphasizing throughout this chapter) the subsequent claim as stated in the Authorized Version: "and [Scripture] is profitable for doctrine, for reproof, for correction, for instruction in righteousness" to the end "that the man [anthrōpos] of God may be perfect, thoroughly furnished unto all good works."[17] The point to emphasize here is that the doxological modality of reading Scripture as a means of grace involves formative dimensions. We are shaped by the work of the Holy Spirit when we attend patiently and attentively to the Bible as Holy Writ.

Reducing Scripture

Both the terms "canon" and "means of grace" help situate Scripture within the specific context of God's sanctifying work. Providentially,

16. Knight, *Presence of God*, 12.
17. Wesley, "Means of Grace," 388, quoting 2 Tim. 3:16–17 KJV.

God's Spirit led the canonization process to give to the church a collection of texts for its spiritual nourishment and growth. Furthermore, God has given us Scripture as a means of grace to help us along in the Christian journey. In reading this text, the church has repeatedly heard the voice of the living God beckoning, challenging, awakening, and transforming it. With such a rich dynamic at work, why is Scripture often neglected as a theological category? And tied to this, why is the Bible frequently used in a reductively utilitarian fashion?

Much of the onus on this score is related to the intellectual imaginaries of Scripture's readers. When people come to the Bible, they do not abandon their ways of thinking and interpreting. Quite the contrary, they come to this text with expectations and tendencies that reflect their immediate environs. These expectations and tendencies relate not only to how they read the Bible but also to what they come to assume about the Bible's character and role, and these are often determined by their wider commitments to and beliefs about how truth coheres. In other words, one's worldview is not incidental to one's reading practices and thus to the way one engages the Bible.

Such are the dynamics related to understanding Scripture as a feeder or resource for theological reflection. For many who are inclined to think that this is how knowledge works, Scripture provides the "base materials" for theological thinking: one collects the facts or data and goes on to compile them in meaningful ways. For some Christians, Scripture presents the facts of faith, and theologians are to compile these meaningfully, coherently, and systematically. Charles Hodge, one of the "Old Princeton" divines, took such an approach to Scripture.[18] In this, he had both antecedents and descendants who followed such conventions of thought.

Those who are inclined to think of Scripture as simply a source for theology tend to be Protestants of a particular sort. Of course, Protestantism found it important to elevate Scripture epistemically in its efforts to correct a particular ecclesial formation, the Roman Catholic Church of the sixteenth century. This kind of privileging is sometimes associated with the *sola Scriptura* tag, for the running assumption here is that Scripture is solely reliable and trustworthy in the

---

18. See Hodge, *Systematic Theology*, 1:1–10.

establishment of a faithful and true Christianity. Human traditions, customs, judgments, and the like are deemed to be open to fallibility, but Protestants find recourse in Scripture: as the word of God, Scripture is stable and reliable for knowing God's will and purposes.

Within this paradigm, Scripture functions as foundational to the theological task. Scripture is pressured, then, to serve epistemic purposes, and this role becomes significantly and solely associated with Scripture. This casting of Scripture overshadows, maybe not explicitly but certainly through usage, its identity as canon and a means of grace. As a result, Scripture retains a place of privilege largely at the epistemic level, and as such, its theological character is neglected. Even terms such as "perspicuity" and "sufficiency" can be pressed for use within this confining paradigm. Such terms can be understood, not as qualities of a theological category (as they certainly were in various dogmatic proposals), but as characteristics of an epistemic category.

Any number of factors could be identified as prompting this shift. For instance, formal biblical study migrated from the church and monastery to the university in a way that relativized the interpreter's location and aims. Also, knowledge at this time was increasingly mathematized and shaped by empirical methodologies so that a person progressed in the creation of knowledge by the establishment of certain principles or axioms that one could then test, employ, and extend in a variety of settings and circumstances so as to form the basis for subsequent claims. Scripture shifted from being revelatory to overwhelming the dogmatic category of revelation, thereby becoming the first topic of choice methodologically when Protestant theologies were written or statements of faith formulated. The most significant culprit of this shift was a morphing of the hermeneutical process altogether so that a gulf was created between text (with its various characteristics and qualities) and readers (including their identities and motives). The gulf was achievable through a collapse and conflation of the text with the practice of interpretation. In a sense, the text became self-interpreting and clear on its own terms and within its own boundaries. The consequence of this move was that the text was understood as not needing a community of interpretation for its meaning to be understood and its purposes to be realized; people just needed to attend to "what was there" in some commonsensical kind of way. Without the communal aspect, a deliberative mechanism for discerning the Spirit's promptings was not deemed necessary. Through such developments, a democratization of the interpretive process ensued. Each believer was left to his or her own conscience to understand God's holy word. If pressed, the assumption was that the human conscience was guided by the internal witness of the Holy Spirit, but explicitly the process was deemed more so an act stemming from a hermeneutical positivism: people simply read and noted what was in the text already. Such an interpretive outlook yielded innumerable factions and a plethora of ecclesial divisions as a result. In light of these, one could postulate a link between a certain species of scriptural foundationalism and the Protestant invention of denominationalism—no appeals process was available to negotiate rival and competing interpretations. Rather than questioning the epistemic conditions that led to such divisiveness, many simply proliferated the divisions, all the while claiming their interpretation as the "right" one. Of course, such outcomes work against the unity Christians are to have in Christ, but they also contribute to an impoverished account of Scripture's character and role among the faithful.

Moving Forward

In light of these past developments, we seek in this volume to explore the theological category of Scripture, and we do so with the outright recognition that many of the contemporary ways Scripture is deployed and understood collectively represent a problematic reduction of Scripture's ontology and teleology. We recognize this situation as partially stemming from identifiable political, cultural, and philosophical shifts that have taken place in the history of the West. These factors make a dogmatic account of Scripture difficult to sustain. Overall, these outcomes debilitate the role and function of Scripture in the lives of the faithful. If Scripture is simply an epistemological foundation or criterion, then people may employ it as a specific means for a particular end that can ultimately be unrelated to the catechetical task—that is, "for teaching, for reproof, for correction, and for training in righteousness, so that everyone who

belongs to God may be proficient, equipped for every good work"
(2 Tim. 3:16–17).

We wish to move past these unhelpful determinations to give a
more bountiful and rich account of Scripture's role and place among
the reading faithful. However one answers the questions with which
we began this chapter—What is Scripture? What is its purpose?—the
results will inevitably shape what can ensue as a theological characterization or dogmatic treatment of the Bible. For us, Scripture as an
auxiliary of the Holy Spirit is providentially shaped and constituted
within the church to aid in this community's ongoing sanctification
and formation as it aims to be faithful to the memory, presence,
and return of the risen One.[19] Scripture is an important auxiliary
no doubt, but it is one of several that the Spirit employs to shape a
people's character and witness over time.[20] The task before us is to
reclaim Scripture's character and function within the church in ac-
cordance with its God-granted purpose of building up the faithful.
Such aims will no doubt influence what we deem as fitting and helpful in our speech regarding Holy Scripture, including the metaphors,
images, and analogies we pursue toward the realization of these ends.

---

19. For an elaboration of this more functional and expansive pneumatology of
Scripture, see Castelo's engagement with Wall's theology of Scripture (Castelo, "Inspiration as Providence," 69–81).

20. William Abraham and his collaborators refer to these materials as constituting
a "canonical heritage" that includes the episcopacy, church councils, creeds, and so
forth; see Abraham, Vickers, and Van Kirk, *Canonical Theism*.

2

Speaking of Scripture

In the previous chapter, we entertained a discussion related to what Scripture is and the holy ends and purposes commensurate with its identity. These claims are basic but nevertheless often muted in conversations related to Scripture's authority. As professors who teach general education classes in a Christian liberal arts university, we often see among our students an inability to engage these questions critically and constructively. For many, Scripture's role in theology and in the church is evident: it is a source, a foundation, a rule, or a warrant. As important as these depictions are, they nevertheless shortchange Scripture. The Bible is much more than a regulator of what is orthodox or a basis for theological and philosophical beliefs. As the church's book, Holy Scripture is a canon and a means of grace by and through which believers come to see God and are shaped and transformed into God's purposes.

This depiction of Scripture's ontology and teleology requires a certain kind of conceptual and linguistic framing. For the point to register, it needs a particular kind of expression. Sundry possibilities exist in this regard, and the choices ultimately do matter, for how believers speak of Scripture is largely determinative of the manner in which Scripture functions in their lives. This point about conceptual and linguistic framing is true in a general sense: The way we come to describe or categorize something tends to determine its status and reality for us. For instance, if we describe an occurrence as a "tragedy," we come to hear and associate different things than those that naturally come with the term "challenge." A tragedy raises associations with loss or absurdity, whereas a challenge can mean a difficulty but also an opportunity. In parallel form, if one uses the language of "foundation" or "revelation" to talk about Scripture, ideas will come to mind that are different from the ones that would occur with the terms "canon" or "means of grace." In sum, speech practices related to Scripture's identity and purposes require probing; each category or term depicts something different, and given the understanding of Scripture's nature and ends presented here, some ways are more helpful than others in communicating that specific vision.

This chapter aims to analyze and critique a particular way of speaking of Scripture and securing its authority that is quite popular among some theologians and confessional traditions, what we will label the "incarnational" or "Christ-Scripture" analogy. As Stephen Fowl notes, this analogy has an especially modern pedigree in terms of its extension and application.[1] We wish to show how it fails at a number of points to register Scripture as a canon and as a means of grace that contributes to the formation of faithful readers. Our contention is that the incarnational analogy is not adequate for promoting the vision of Scripture's ontology and teleology we have proposed so far. As popular as it is, it cannot ultimately account for what Scripture is and what it is for.

Theological Speech as Analogical Speech

The tradition of Christian intellectual inquiry has long recognized that language is limited in its capacity to illuminate and elaborate the significance of the faith. Part of the difficulty relates simply to the capacity of language itself: language can both convey and obscure since it is both employed and constructed by humans to communicate meaning. These concerns relate to language in general, but they are especially worth considering in terms of God-talk (that is, the

---

1. See Fowl, *Theological Interpretation of Scripture*, 2.

names, images, metaphors, and actions attributed to God in Christian discursive practices). God is unlike any other object one can consider because God is not just another object we come to know. While it is generally true that part of the knowing process in terms of the subject-object interface is that the subject wields a certain kind of determining privilege in the process itself, this kind of privilege is basically unworkable when talk of beholding God properly and faithfully is at play. After all, at a fundamental level, we could not even *be* apart from the divine initiative.

Given this general recognition of the shape of theological knowledge and speech, we must further specify that both univocal and "purely"[2] equivocal speech practices are unworkable options in God-talk. When Christians speak of God, they do so in a mediated form. Their linguistic choices do not have a one-to-one correspondence with the God they are seeking to account for; therefore, at work here is definitely not a univocal dynamic. However, Christian speech is not thoroughly equivocal either. Christians hold that their speech can be fitting and true given their conviction that the God they worship is manifest and knowable. The divine self-presentation creates a vital link between God and creatures—God ultimately makes Godself knowable so that creaturely God-talk can be something other than strictly anthropologically derivative and oriented. Therefore, contrary to the views of some modern thinkers, theology ultimately need not be anthropology.[3] Believers are able to operate with a certain level of confidence that their speech about God can be reliable and fitting.

What keeps God-talk logically from being neither univocal nor equivocal is an analogical interval. Because God's self-presentation is available within the bounds of the economy, it is a true but limited revelation. Whatever one wishes to make of the divine self-presentation

2. The importance of the term "purely" rests on a point made by Thomas Aquinas in *Summa Theologiae* 1.13.5. Equivocation is in some measured way involved with the employment of analogies since the comparison of two *different* things is at stake. Nevertheless, the assumption of God-talk is that a comparison can in fact be made, and fruitfully so, on the basis of the divine gratuity and self-presentation: because God allows and makes possible such speech, it cannot be cast simply as "pure" equivocation.

3. Many subscribe to this point out of a number of atheistic assumptions, but one prominent figure within this view is Ludwig Feuerbach.

for a theological grammar, a basic claim has to be that God's disclosure is always at work within a broader horizon of closure. This affirmation is not an indictment of God's character (for instance, by suggesting that God teasingly or reluctantly makes Godself known) but simply a recognition that the Creator and the creation, the Savior and the saved, are two separate, nonidentical realities (and so the language of "interval") that in turn are related in a particular way (a point suggested by the modifier "analogical").

This claim of God's self-disclosure always taking place within a context of closure can be summed up another way: God is ultimately a self-revealing mystery. One has to be careful with the language of mystery in theological reflection because it can be used as a way of halting a discussion or avoiding an issue that thoroughly reorients a conversation or logic.[4] The appeal to mystery could be entangled with many problematic assumptions, fears, and biases that lurk in the background of a particular theological exercise; if this is the case, then the notion of mystery is being mishandled and misapplied. Rather than being used as a rhetorical strategy of deferral or avoidance, the claim that God is a self-revealed mystery suggests that at a fundamental level God is both beyond our imagination and yet very much active in our world (and God is not diminished by being so). The category of mystery within theological reflection can significantly shape the way theological speakers think about, evaluate, and sustain their work by orienting them in a basic, primordial way *outside* of themselves to the God of their wonder and delight.

Analogizing Scripture

What has been entertained broadly about theological speech can be applied to many topics of the Christian faith, including Scripture. When Christians reflect theologically about Scripture, they attempt to speak of a collection of texts that God uses to form God's people. And given that God reveals Godself through Scripture, the manner in which believers account for Scripture can take any number of

---

4. A recent effort that makes a compelling attempt to invigorate and yet properly cast the term "mystery" is Boyer and Hall, *Mystery of God*.

expressions and forms. One image, model, or figure of speech cannot do justice to Scripture's role since this role is intrinsically tied to the operations and self-manifestation of the triune God, which in turn cannot be encapsulated within a singular heading or notion. Therefore, in the effort to speak of Scripture's significance within the common life of faith, believers can resort to any number of metaphors, symbols, and analogies since ultimately they are attempting to account for God's work through Scripture. Just as in theological speech generally, so in speaking about Scripture: it requires attentiveness, surveillance, and ongoing evaluation and testing, for some names, symbols, or analogies can come to obscure more than illuminate, to obfuscate more than reveal.

Such work of analyzing and attending to the ways Christians speak of Scripture is at some level counterintuitive. We have said this already: as pronounced as the authority of Scripture is for many Christians, these same believers often are not trained to be versatile and critical with the ways they think or talk about Scripture. The metaphors, figures of speech, and tropes they use to describe Scripture are sometimes simply picked up and perpetuated without significant evaluation. However, by attending to Scripture in a myriad of ways—for instance, when referring to its performances as "canonical" or when describing it as functioning as a "means of grace" (as we have done in the previous chapter)—believers can cultivate an awareness of Scripture's role within the economy of salvation history. Scripture's place in the outworking of God's purposes over time is dynamic and multivalent. The richness of this vision suggests that a manner of speaking and elaboration that is both critical and creative is in order. More ways of speaking of Scripture mean more opportunities for the fullness of God's self-presentation to register in a community's social imaginary.[5] There is no need—in fact it is perilous—to engage in "metaphoric myopia."[6]

5. Our idea of a "social imaginary" is based on the work of Charles Taylor, who has argued that our intellectual constructions of certain subjects, such as Scripture, are never detached from the social world in which that particular subject is received and employed. In this sense, we would argue that any theological construction of Scripture is finally unintelligible apart from the partnerships and performances that are forged within its ecclesial world.
6. We owe this phrase to Van De Walle, *Rethinking Holiness*, 117.

As Denys Turner once remarked to his students, "If you want to do theology well, then, for God's sake get your metaphors as thoroughly mixed as you can."[7] The analogical nature of theological speech means that tropes and constructs surrounding the means God uses to accomplish God's purposes are modifiable and can be revised through the prayerful exchanges and critical deliberations of the worshiping faithful. We are arguing that speaking of Scripture should be one such case.

Introducing the Incarnational Analogy

In the spirit of this call to be vigilant and nimble with metaphors and analogies generally, and with those related to Scripture particularly, we can now come back to the Christ-Scripture or incarnational analogy and examine its problems. It has made its way into a number of works, figures, and traditions.[8] In fact, it is the kind of analogy that many intuitively make when thinking about Scripture in theological terms. At its core, the incarnational analogy suggests that Scripture can be thought of similarly to Christ, the one whom Christians proclaim to be God in the flesh. In the case of both Scripture and Christ, espousers of this analogy say, divine and human natures are identifiable in each. Just as these qualifiers are applied to Christ paradoxically as set forth by the Council of Chalcedon, so too, it is said, they can be extended to the Bible. The conclusion is that Scripture, like Christ, can be talked about as "divine" and "human." In speaking this way, purveyors of this approach may not directly cite Christology as their orienting perspective. However, in such cases the logic is implicit: an echo of Chalcedon is detectable.

---

7. Turner, "Apophaticism, Idolatry, and the Claims of Reason," 18. Turner's approach, based on the way of negation of pseudo-Dionysius, is to set forth a dialectical tension between prolixity and silence so that "we talk about God in as many ways as possible, even in as many conflicting ways as possible, that we use up the whole stock-in-trade of imagery and discourse in our possession, so as thereby to discover ultimately the inadequacy of all of it" (17).

8. For instance, this analogy is so prominent that Michael Gorman is compelled to include it in his introductory text to exegesis as the first of eight "principles" for the theological interpretation of Scripture; see *Elements of Biblical Exegesis*, 149–50.

What are the warrants for making this particular analogy? Some people reference biblical themes to justify it. One prominent example is the depiction of Jesus the Christ as the divine Word or *logos* in terms of what Telford Work calls the "Analogy of the Word."[9] For instance, according to the Fourth Gospel, the Word who was in the beginning with God and was God's very self (John 1:1) is also the Word who became flesh and lived among creatures (v. 14). Whatever the source of inspiration for this Gospel writer's choice of images, the move to depict Christ in terms of *logos* inevitably creates a link between it and other articulations involving a metaphysical *logos*.[10] Since Sacred Scripture is textual, linguistic, and so the stuff of "words" as well, the Gospel's depiction of the incarnate Word is ready-made for those who wish to underwrite the theological significance of Holy Writ as analogical to Christ. Whatever their proportional arrangements, Christ and Scripture are potential analogues when cast under the heading of *logoi*, or "words."

Perhaps an even more powerful example is provided by the book of Hebrews, in which the conception of divine speech includes auditions of the Son's incarnation (Heb. 1:1–3) and Scripture's quotations, which are frequently introduced as divine *logoi* (e.g., 1:5; 2:11; 3:7; 5:5; and others). As such, the famous text about the living and animating "word of God" (see 4:12–13), which concludes the letter's initial exposition on the failure of the wilderness generation to hear and heed God's voice, includes both Scripture (Heb. 3:7–11, quoting Ps. 95:7–11) and the apostolic witness of the incarnate Son (2:3). Here both Scripture and Son are instantiations of God's word in the divine economy.

We could extend the examples to include other biblical warrants, but as we will show, the warrants sustaining this analogy are not simply biblical. Other forces can be at work in making it appealing, ones that relate to questions of authority, methodological privilege, and so forth. Nevertheless, at this point, we are simply stressing that for many people, Christ and Scripture form a natural pairing, one that is justified and exploited in sundry ways.

9. Work, *Living and Active*, 15–27.
10. Early church writers, particularly from the era of the Apologists, were quick to draw this connection and in turn produced an approach labeled "Logos Christology."

Purposes and Examples of the Incarnational Analogy

What are the ends or purposes for sustaining the incarnational analogy? Why would people expend the effort to make this particular connection between the incarnate Word and the written Word? From one end, one could guess that the gesture aims to stress the authority of Scripture—that the Bible is *God's* Word—while not denying its origins in human circumstances. Plenty of Christians, particularly Protestants, would find such an approach quite favorable. For instance, early in his *Institutes*, John Calvin claims Scripture's "divine nature" quite directly: "Hence the Scriptures obtain full authority among believers only when men regard them as having sprung from heaven, as if there the living words of God were heard."[11] A bit later he adds, "But because the church recognizes Scripture to be the truth of its own God, as a pious duty it unhesitatingly venerates Scripture."[12] Of course, Calvin's logic is quite nuanced, and one feature of his theology of Scripture that is sometimes missed is his strong regard for a pneumatological account of Scripture's production (inspiration) *and* its performance (illumination).[13] Nevertheless, Protestants historically have had a penchant for stressing Scripture's authority in terms of its role in holding accountable and judging human traditions, and that kind of work would be problematic to associate with another human production. Scripture's "divine" character, then, would be important to register for such purposes, as Calvin and others have done.[14] Within such an environment, one can see how the incarnational analogy could highlight Scripture's authority because of its "divine" origins and characteristics, while not necessarily denying

11. Calvin, *Institutes* 1.7.1, p. 74.
12. Calvin, *Institutes* 1.7.2, p. 76.
13. Calvin, *Institutes* 1.7.4, pp. 78–80.
14. One prominent example we will not be considering here is Karl Barth, whom Work believes is in the background of some modern variations on this theme (see *Living and Active*, 19–20, and his more extensive treatment on 67–100). The Barthian point in question is the threefold form of the word of God (*Church Dogmatics* I). Interestingly, Barth's son, Markus Barth, raised reservations along these lines in *Conversation with the Bible*. Work's broad survey proves very helpful here; see *Living and Active*, 19–32. In terms of Work's project itself, we find his efforts to be commendable on several scores as he too attempts to highlight Scripture's role within the economy of salvation.

its "human" factors but perhaps casting them as secondary or even ancillary to some degree.

The examples Fowl raises to illustrate the analogy's usage bend in a different direction from the above tendency. These are cases that reflect not simply a certain worldview (such as modernity) but also a particular location—namely, the academy generally and the biblical studies guild in particular. The push here comes from scholars hoping to stress the ways Scripture should not be given a pass with regard to formal investigation simply because it is a book labeled "inspired" and "holy" by Christian believers. In other words, how should Scripture be analyzed given that it is a "human" production and expression? Whatever one wishes to say about its "divine" character, they would argue, Scripture's "human" qualities cannot be denied: it is textual and linguistic and thereby embedded contextually and culturally. On the basis of these factors, Scripture can be described as having a "human nature." This camp would say that denying this feature of Scripture's constitution has been and continues to be a hermeneutical mistake that causes the Bible to lose its objective quality as a significant "other" to be engaged.

Fowl points to the work of Ernst Käsemann as an example, citing Käsemann's belief that the admission of Scripture's materiality warrants the use and preserves the legitimacy of historical-critical scrutiny of the Bible.[15] On Käsemann's account, failure to examine Scripture in this way would amount to a capitulation to that christological problem known as docetism, the family of heresies and tendencies that cannot recognize the authentic physicality of Christ's body.[16] The danger detected through this concern is precisely an overspiritualization of material realities—whether Christ or Scripture—and the compromised ways these realities may be

15. Fowl's source for Käsemann's views is "Vom theologischen Recht historisch-kritischer Exegese."

16. A debate has ensued on this point, one related to an assessment of the theological character of Käsemann's methodological orientation as well as the difficulty of circumscribing the term "docetism." See Adam, "Docetism, Käsemann, and Christology," and Strawn's article with the same title. Whichever account is most convincing, both Adam and Strawn agree that historical-critical methodologies are inadequate on their own as hermeneutical tools, a point potentially lost on those who follow Käsemann's impulses.

engaged as a result. Given its "human" qualities, so the approach goes, the Bible should be read with the same degree of historical, literary, and cultural scrutiny that other ancient texts would require. Working on these assumptions, some have even made it axiomatic to say that the Bible should be read as "any other book."[17] They would say that its status as the sacred text of Christianity does not make the Bible exempt from the demands of sound, thorough, and critical investigation.

Certain Roman Catholics have followed this line of thinking and have made a similar case from their own ecclesial setting.[18] The posture is detectable in the 1993 text from the Pontifical Biblical Commission titled "Document on the Interpretation of the Bible in the Church."[19] The self-proclaimed aim of the document is "to indicate the paths most appropriate for arriving at an interpretation of the Bible as faithful as possible to *its character, both human and divine*." In response to what they find problematic with synchronic and "spiritual" readings of the Bible, the document's authors believe that "the historical-critical method is the indispensable method for the scientific study of the meaning of ancient texts."[20] This method is critical, they say, because "it operates with the help of scientific criteria that seek to be as objective as possible. . . . [The method] aims to make accessible to the modern reader the meaning of biblical texts."[21] In its conclusion, the document offers the following mandate: "The eternal Word became incarnate at a precise period of history, within a clearly defined cultural and social environment. Anyone who desires to understand the Word of God should humbly seek it out there where

17. Variants of this phrasing are usually attributed to Benjamin Jowett; see the historical and critical analysis of this theme in Moberly, "'Interpret the Bible like Any Other Book'?"

18. Other Roman Catholic examples not surveyed here are the papal encyclical *Divino Afflante Spiritu* (1943) and Nichols, *Shape of Catholic Theology*, both of which are considered in Work, *Living and Active*, 20–21.

19. We were directed to this document by Ayres and Fowl, "(Mis)reading the Face of God." Although we tend to believe that Ayres and Fowl overstate the place of the Christ-Scripture analogy within this document, we are generally in agreement with the direction of their concerns.

20. Pontifical Biblical Commission, "Interpretation of the Bible in the Church," 248–49 (emphasis added).

21. Pontifical Biblical Commission, "Interpretation of the Bible in the Church," 251.

it has made itself visible and accept to this end the necessary help of human knowledge."[22]

In pressing into the nuances of both cases above, further efforts have tried to curb the most difficult aspects of such proposals. Brent Strawn's reaction to A. K. M. Adam's article on Käsemann makes this point by casting Käsemann as attempting a middle road between Rudolf Bultmann (and his demythologization project) and pietistic readings of Scripture as he speaks about Scripture's "human" character.[23] Likewise, "Interpretation of the Bible in the Church" is prefaced by then Cardinal Ratzinger so as to suggest that the document is at least implicitly in continuity with broader theological claims, including the confession that God is the genuine author of Scripture and that historical-critical methods may be taken too far in theological reflection.[24] The document's stated aim is "to examine all the methods likely to contribute effectively to the task of making more available the riches contained in biblical texts . . . [in order] that the Word of God may become more and more the spiritual nourishment of the members of the People of God, the source for them of a life of faith, of hope, and of love—and indeed a light for all humanity."[25]

Another proponent of this analogy hails from a different ecclesial camp than those surveyed thus far, yet one sees similarities between his proposal and others. Peter Enns, an Old Testament scholar within the American evangelical fold, begins his book *Inspiration and Incarnation* by saying that, however the church "*fleshes out* its doctrine of Scripture," it will "always have somewhat of a provisional quality

22. Pontifical Biblical Commission, "Interpretation of the Bible in the Church," 313. Interestingly enough, the document resembles Jowett's claim in this way: "As an analytical method [the historical-critical method] studies the biblical text in the same fashion as it would study any other ancient text and comments upon it as an expression of human discourse" (251).

23. Adam, "Docetism, Käsemann, and Christology"; Strawn, "Docetism, Käsemann, and Christology."

24. Pontifical Biblical Commission, "Interpretation of the Bible in the Church," 244.

25. Pontifical Biblical Commission, "Interpretation of the Bible in the Church," 249. A footnoted reference to Pope Paul VI, *Dei Verbum* (available at http://www.vatican.va/archive/hist_councils/ii_vatican_council/documents/vat-ii_const_19651118_dei-verbum_en.html) is made at this point.

to it."[26] One senses that part of his aim is to reconceive how biblical authority is openly negotiated in evangelical circles, especially in relation to their assumptions and expectations. Enns claims the following as his book's overarching commitment: "*As Christ is both God and human, so is the Bible.* In other words, we are to think of the Bible analogously to how Christians think about Jesus. Christians confess that Jesus is both God and human at the same time. . . . This way of thinking of Christ is analogous to thinking about the Bible. In the same way that Jesus is . . . both God and human, the Bible is also a divine and human book."[27] Enns believes that an incarnational analogy for Scripture, one that acknowledges its "divine" and "human" natures, will help evangelicals come to terms with Scripture's particularity as a historical and cultural phenomenon. In other words, the Christ-Scripture or incarnational analogy for Enns helps create space for the advancements in historical-critical biblical scholarship (especially with regard to the Old Testament) that he believes have been selectively considered or neglectfully avoided by many evangelicals for far too long. While not giving up on Protestant commitments to the authority of Scripture, Enns wishes to highlight the other side of the paradox—the human side—for the sake of placing modern biblical studies and evangelical commitments on friendlier terms. Enns stresses that the pursuit of this goal is ultimately for the sake of building up evangelical faith itself.[28]

Limits of the Incarnational Analogy

As the above examples show, the incarnational analogy is utilized for a number of purposes, many of which, it should be noted, are quite helpful on their own. We believe that Christians should account for Holy Scripture in ways that help secure its practical authority in

---

26. Enns, *Inspiration and Incarnation*, 2 (emphasis original).

27. Enns, *Inspiration and Incarnation*, 5 (emphasis original).

28. In a postscript to the tenth anniversary edition of his text and in response to his critics, Enns emphasizes the analogical nature of what he has offered, affirming that he does not believe the Bible to be ontologically human and divine the way Jesus is. Enns, *Inspiration and Incarnation*, 172. As important as this clarification is, we do not believe that this acknowledgment adequately shapes his overall argument.

forming Christian faith and life. When believers read the words of Jesus, hear the exhortations of Paul, come to learn of the covenant between Yahweh and Israel, and so on, they are not simply encountering entertaining stories or useful life lessons. Rather, the text shapes the very warp and woof of Christian identity and tradition. The use of analogies, including the incarnational analogy, can invigorate the role and significance of Scripture in people's lives.

Furthermore, even though Scripture is authoritative in matters of faith, it still must be analyzed and scrutinized with the most compelling tools available—whether historical-critical, hermeneutical, or otherwise. Much can be gleaned from the biblical text when one attends to it with the full panoply of resources available from the fields of biblical criticism and interpretation. These resources need not be considered the enemies of faith; rather, they can aid and deepen faith by helping Scripture's readers account for the contexts and challenges associated with specific texts. Faith is not the enemy of particularity, contingency, and perspective; rather, faith comes to be and is affirmed within such conditions. Likewise, the Bible's authority and its character as a textual entity can be understood as working hand in hand.[29]

We also wish to repeat that we are committed to a diversity of analogies for thinking and speaking about Scripture, and this for a number of reasons. No single analogy can account for all that Christians wish to say about the way God works through Scripture. Overreliance on one analogy can in turn reify or complicate unhelpful vantage points and tendencies and can cause matters to become skewed. Furthermore, at some level the adequacy of analogies depends on how one applies them and the goals for which they are used. For instance, Enns's orienting vision is at points similar to our own,[30] and he presumably strives to make a case for this vision by extending

---

29. For a helpful proposal toward this end, see Billings, *Word of God for the People of God*, 54–61.

30. Take this quote, for example: "The primary purpose of Scripture is for the church to eat and drink its contents in order to understand better who God is, what he has done, and what it means to be his people, redeemed in the crucified and risen Son. Such an understanding of the purpose of Scripture—as a means of grace for the church—actually opens up possibilities of interpretation instead of closing them." Enns, *Inspiration and Incarnation*, 160. We could not agree more with this statement. However, Enns's approach is not so much doctrinal as it is textual and

the incarnational analogy itself. Therefore it would be tempting for us, given this affinity, to say that the incarnational analogy is simply "another way" to promote what we are saying of Scripture's role and place in the economy of God's manifest work of salvation.

However, whereas we are committed to a diversity of analogies, we also stress that some analogies are more helpful than others for communicating certain claims while keeping others at bay. In other words, we believe that "not all analogies are created equal." And in this regard, we find the incarnational analogy inherently and structurally flawed for communicating what we believe about Scripture's ontology and teleology and for thinking of Scripture as a canon and means of grace. In fact, we propose that this analogy should be put to rest. It simply complicates and obfuscates too many crucial matters in the wake of its extension. Why would we propose such a direct and drastic course of action?

First, we believe that using the incarnation of Christ as the basis for analogy construction takes away from the uniqueness of the Christ-event itself. We are inclined to stress just how radical the incarnation of the Second Person of the Trinity is, not simply for the life of faith, but also for the very constitution of the cosmos itself. Contrary to Enns, we cannot hold that "Christ's incarnation is analogous to Scripture's 'incarnation,'"[31] for there is nothing in the Christian vision of reality approximately comparable to the unique event in which the Creator has become the created. Now of course, yes, there is a paradox at work in this event, one that the Council of Chalcedon attempted (however adequately) to account for through the language of "two natures." Yes, both Christ and Scripture can be spoken of as "the word of God." However, perpetuating this analogy has the

---

historical, which, in our opinion, makes his use of the incarnational analogy somewhat underdeveloped and thus susceptible to misunderstanding and misapplication.

31. Enns, *Inspiration and Incarnation*, 6. Again, we wish to be fair to Enns. At another point, he draws an important distinction: "The Bible is God's word in written form; Christ is God's word in human form. . . . The written word bears witness to the incarnate word, Christ. And what gives the written word its unity is not simply the words on the page, but the incarnate word who is more than simply the sum of biblical parts. He is the one through whom heaven and earth—including the Bible itself—were created" (110). As we have said previously, we simply wish to see more of this from Enns so that his proposals could be on surer theological footing.

possibility of relativizing Jesus's incarnation amid other assumed "incarnations." At some level, the analogy occludes unique features related to God's self-presentation in Christ. It also potentially complicates a proper evaluation of Scripture itself, which leads us to our next point.

Second, we believe the incarnational analogy has the potential to set up a trajectory of misconstrued contrasts. In fact, this is what we detect to be happening with many uses of this analogy. On one side, some may functionally divinize Scripture by tying it too closely to revelation or to God's self-presentation. In fact, John Webster believes one "can scarcely avoid divinizing the Bible" when perpetuating this analogy from this angle since this move would advance an "ontological identity" between, on the one hand, the godlike propositions of the Bible and, on the other hand, Christ, who is God in the flesh.[32] Yes, Christians agree that Scripture is a living and animating word (see Heb. 4:12)—God works through it to judge, comfort, and heal us. And yet it is helpful to remember (as obvious as it may seem) that the Bible is not God; Scripture is not a triune person or the Trinity itself. Therefore, speaking of Scripture as divine has its limitations, ones that if ignored could lead to idolatrous ends.

On the other side, Jesus and the Bible do have to be contextualized in various ways. The cultural conventions at work in their respective situatedness as well as their reflected languages, thought paradigms, and imaginaries all need to be accounted for relative to their understanding and reception within our own historical and cultural embeddedness. But again, stressing "human natures" here seems misplaced. For one thing, Christ's incarnation sets up a dynamic not simply of identification but also of solidarity with the human condition so that a particular kind of answer is offered in response to the question, *Cur deus homo?* Why did God become human? The affirmation of Jesus's human nature—of his living, breathing *flesh*—comes out of a metanarrative rich with soteriological specification. Certainly Christ's contextual embeddedness is necessary to consider, but that point seems to be simply one aspect of all that is at work when people claim that he is "fully human." Put another way, the christological

---

32. Webster, *Holy Scripture*, 23.

affirmation of a human nature does not merely mean accounting for the historical and cultural embeddedness of a historical figure; rather, speaking of Christ as human is simply a different kind of claim than saying that Scripture is human, given the theological stakes of Christ's incarnation itself.

Third and finally, the prospect of a contrastive or dyadic presentation for something that is meant to be "useful for teaching, for reproof, for correction, and for training in righteousness" (2 Tim. 3:16) is at some point problematic. Certainly paradoxes are important for understanding the Christian faith. However, paradoxes must be grounded in something larger and broader so that the tensions expressed in them do not lead to blatant nonsense. For instance, in the case of the incarnation of Christ, the claim that Christ is divine and human is a confession grounded in many experiences, claims, and texts. At some level, it is best conceptualized as a conclusory— rather than initiatory—understanding. Ayres and Fowl relate as much when they say, "The classical formula that Christ had two natures in one person is not made in isolation, but within a complex theological matrix. The theology of Christ's two natures is intimately interwoven with assertions about God's educative economy in and through the person of Christ and with assertions about God's economy of restoration and redemption in Christ."[33] If Scripture is spoken of as "divine" and "human," not only do the above reservations stand, but the further question arises: What is keeping this paradox grounded in some broader, orienting framework? What, after all, is Scripture's corresponding "complex theological matrix" that allows the incarnational analogy to make good theological sense? Without an extensive treatment of this more fundamental orienting perspective, one feature of the paradox may be excessively or conveniently highlighted over another. And if so, the paradox could subsequently break down. As most of the examples above show, this is exactly what has often happened with the analogy's utilization in conversations related to Scripture.

What is needed is a different approach from the ones on offer by proponents of the incarnational or Christ-Scripture analogy. Again,

33. Ayres and Fowl, "(Mis)Reading the Face of God," 523.

multiple images and analogies are worthwhile in accounting for Scripture's identity and role among the faithful; however, the incarnational
analogy inherently introduces a number of exceedingly overburden-
ing complications that make it less than ideal for such work. From
our end, we press for an alternative analogy, one that can be labeled
the "church-Scripture" or "ecclesial" analogy, and we will extend its
warrants and its orienting "complex theological matrix" in terms of
the economy of sanctification.

Introducing the Church-Scripture Analogy

In his important "dogmatic sketch" of Holy Scripture, the late John
Webster offers a way forward from the impasse associated with the
implementation of the incarnational analogy. Rather than continuing the disjunctive approach of speaking of Scripture's human and
divine natures, Webster offers "an account of what Holy Scripture
is in the saving economy of God's loving and regenerative self-
communication."[34] The shift indicated by this quote is important.
Rather than substantiating the categories of divine and human as they
apply to Scripture, Webster is interested in offering a doctrinal understanding of Scripture in which the triune God's presence and purposes
are first and foremost for thinking of Scripture in a theological way.
This approach to Holy Scripture implies at least the following three
things: the interplay of Scripture's functions and ends, this interplay
within God's economy, and Scripture's addressees.

For Webster, one begins a dogmatics of Scripture by recognizing
"its role in God's self-communication, that is, the acts of Father, Son,
and Spirit which establish and maintain that saving fellowship with
humankind in which God makes himself known to us and by us."[35]
This feature of the dogmatic task was often lost on modernity when
it tended to emphasize the category of revelation as a mechanism
by which to secure its theological purchase epistemically (in what
Webster labels the "hypertrophy of revelation"). This sort of privileging of epistemology and the noetic has had a way of deforming

34. Webster, *Holy Scripture*, 2.
35. Webster, *Holy Scripture*, 8.

and impeding a theological account of revelation,[36] a state of affairs presently remediable through an affirmation of the triune God's presence, activity, and purposes in the world. Revelation generally and the topic of Scripture particularly need not function in some quasi-independent fashion, as they often are narrated within modernity once the presence and work of God are claimed as primordial to these.

Webster believes that speaking of Scripture's holiness and its role in sanctification creates an important way forward from the dualistic impasse of the incarnational analogy we have surveyed thus far. He continues, "In the context of discussing the relation between divine self-revelation and the nature of Holy Scripture, sanctification functions as a middle term, indicating in a general way God's activity of appointing and ordering the creaturely realization of the biblical texts towards the end of the divine self-manifestation."[37] This "middle term" is important for a number of reasons. Webster intentionally chooses sanctification because it is a theme that allows for creaturehood (similar to what we have found of value with the use of the category of "canon" and the process of canonization). As Webster remarks, "At its most basic, the notion [of sanctification] states that the biblical texts are creaturely realities set apart by the triune God to serve his self-presence."[38] Creaturely realities are sanctified when they are set apart and used by God, yet in this process they retain their status as creaturely throughout. In other words, it is *because of* (and not *despite*) their identity as creaturely that people, places, texts, and other materials can be hallowed or sanctified. For purposes of applying this idea to the Bible, one can say that Scripture is holy because it is a creaturely reality put to use by the Holy Trinity for holy ends.

Those holy ends involve the sanctification and healing of Scripture's addressee, which is the church. Webster repeatedly emphasizes that the church is a hearing fellowship, one that exists "outside itself" by being called into existence by the triune God. Scripture's role at

---

36. Although Webster expresses reservations with regard to William Abraham's project in *Canon and Criterion*, both Webster and Abraham can agree on this point related to revelation. See Webster's article-length review "Canon and Criterion."

37. Webster, *Holy Scripture*, 9–10.

38. Webster, *Holy Scripture*, 21.

this juncture is to help incline the church (whether by sacerdotally building it up or prophetically tearing it down) toward attending to God's acts of self-communication: "Holy Scripture serves the spiritually visible, apostolic church as the instrument through which the Spirit breaks and reforms the community."[39] In this light, Webster argues, Scripture serves a soteriological function within the church, a role that would constitute it as a means of grace.[40]

On these points, Scripture is intimately connected to the church, the people of God. As noted in the previous chapter through the discussion of canonization, Scripture comes to be within the context of the church. The church, prompted and led by the Spirit, has made judgments with regard to Scripture so as to make it what it is today (in terms of book order, book choices, numbering, and so on). We confess that Scripture is "Spirit-breathed," but that dynamic takes place and is recognized within the community of faith.

This last point connects Scripture and the church on a second score. The performances of Scripture as a means of grace—its work of teaching, reproving, correcting, and training—have to be on display and operative somewhere, and that "somewhere" is properly understood as the fellowship of the faithful. It is the church that recognizes the Bible as Holy Writ. The church reads Sacred Scripture to encounter within its pages the God whom it confesses and praises, for it is the church that sees Scripture as the means of grace that it is: one of God's elected, ordinary channels by which God conveys to humanity God's saving and sanctifying grace. The church is Scripture's legal address, meaning that Scripture both emerges from and is directed back to the community of faith for its own healing.

This particular pairing of Scripture and the church avoids the pitfalls of the incarnational analogy as documented above. Scripture and the church are very much embedded in their wider cultural and historical contexts, and each bears the distinct stamp of being thoroughly creaturely in its identity. In other words, one cannot label either Scripture or the church as "divine." We believe this pairing helps

---

39. Webster, *Holy Scripture*, 52.

40. Apparently Webster has some reservations with the language of mediation (see *Holy Scripture*, 24–25), but it seems that he would not terribly mind the notion as long as what mediates does not eclipse what is said to be mediated.

in resisting the tendency to functionally divinize Scripture, which is a long-standing problem for some Christians. God can and does present Godself through Scripture and the church, but in this depiction the divine self-presentation can be distinguished from Scripture and the church. With these claims at work, the uniqueness of the incarnation can be preserved along with its correlative implications and effects. Scripture and the church simply represent more proximate—and thus helpful—analogues. And with this pairing, the themes of formation, maturation, and sanctification in the Christian life can be more prominently registered. After all, by emphasizing the ecclesial analogy, we believe that the division between church and academy—a division that often drives the use of the incarnational analogy itself—can be reckoned with head-on. Without apology or excuse, we can stress Scripture's performances among the faithful because we are unabashedly saying that Scripture cannot be understood apart from this community. Scripture is first and foremost the church's book—the word of God for the people of God.

Conclusion

In this chapter, we attempt to reckon with the limits and possibilities of theological language as they pertain to speaking of Scripture as a theological category. We highlight one such tendency—the incarnational analogy—and survey some of its instantiations to show its limits. In its place, we propose an alternative: the church-Scripture or ecclesial analogy. We believe this alternative is more helpful than the incarnational analogy for attending to what we have proposed as Scripture's ontology and teleology. We made some brief comments above in favor of our preferred alternative, but much more work is needed to make a resounding argument in its favor.

That more extensive case is the task of the rest of the book. In the next four chapters (3–6), we will forge a constructive account of our preferred analogy, cued by the confession of the church as "one," "holy," "catholic," and "apostolic" as set forth in the Niceno-Constantinopolitan Creed. These attributes are sometimes referred to as the "marks of the church," and we believe that they could also be thought of as the "marks of Scripture": Scripture too can be spoken of as one, holy, catholic, and apostolic. Each chapter will have a general introduction followed by (1) a dogmatic and practical foray written by Castelo on how the church can be understood as exemplifying the mark in question, (2) a constructive account by Wall that builds on the ecclesiological reflections previously made and applies them analogously to Scripture, and (3) a concluding section that summarizes the chapter's logic and takeaways. A final chapter (7) will touch on Bible-reading practices that can help the faithful extend the church-Scripture or ecclesial analogy more broadly for the sake of tending to Scripture's ontology and teleology.

Unity

We begin our exploration of Scripture's marks by following the same sequence registered by the church's confession of itself: we affirm that the church and Scripture are one. Yet even a cursory review of the church's life and its engagement with its Scripture detects the constant temptation to fracture into various bits and pieces, which often leads to the privileging of one part over all others. Reasons are sometimes offered why this is so, whether as a matter of cultural relevance or of theological priority, but here we focus on a vision of unity that is made possible because the God of Christian confession summons a people to live with "one heart and soul" (Acts 4:32) and inspires their holy text with the aim that they may bear witness to God's life-giving and transformative presence. With regard to the church and Scripture, unity is not a status or an achievement but a function made possible by the Spirit in conformity to Christ.

PRACTICAL AND DOGMATIC CONSIDERATIONS

Of the four ecclesial marks being considered in the present work, the one that is perhaps most egregiously unbearable is the confession of the church's unity. It is blatantly obvious to any observer that the church, the body of Christ's disciples that claims him as Lord, is anything but one and united. Historically and currently, the church has divided time and time again, and often these divisions appear unnecessary and maybe even petty, given the justifications offered. Cultural differences, assertions of power, human pride—these can be what is truly at the basis of particular ecclesial divisions. Furthermore, these schisms have sometimes been the occasion for deep conflict and even violent engagements. In increasingly secularized contexts, this history can only work against the church's witness and mission. An outside observer could ask: If the church is so divided, then is it really a compelling form of human community?

But this question raises some more fundamental considerations. For instance, are there any forms of human community that resemble a kind of idealized sense of unity where everybody believes in the same thing in the same way? Obviously there are not, so is it fair to expect something of the church that is in one sense a human impossibility? At some level, Christians and others should not think of the church as "just another form of human community," and yet at another level, how could the church be otherwise? Within fallen human conditions, people in and out of the church will engage in silly, selfish, and blatantly deplorable activities. The church is called to a higher standard, to be sure, but the difficulty is that the standard does not always play out in day-to-day happenings due to human ignorance, negligence, and yes, sin. And when the standard is so high, as it is in the case of the church, missing the mark of unity becomes all the more scandalous as people point out inconsistencies and blatant hypocrisy.[1]

But what exactly is this standard? What precisely is Christian ecclesial unity? To begin, we should say that, as in the Christian doctrine of God, maybe also in the doctrine of the church: it may be easier to specify what this unity is *not* as a gateway to saying what it is. This general apophatic approach will guide each of the first sections of the chapters devoted to the individual marks. It should help establish some parameters and guidelines for speaking positively of the marks (including this chapter's mark: unity) along trinitarian and missional lines.

1. A work that tackles these challenges head-on is Radner, *Brutal Unity*.

The Church's Unity Is Not Uniformity

Christian unity does not mean uniformity. Here we take "uniformity" to imply a kind of sameness that does away with varying kinds of diversity. The point is registered in Scripture itself: After spelling out some theological claims, Paul proceeds to develop a metaphor by remarking that "the body does not consist of one member but of many" (1 Cor. 12:14). He goes on to say that a foot is not a hand and yet belongs to the human body; the same is true of the ear and the nose. Each has its function. Paul summarizes: "If all were a single member, where would the body be? As it is, there are many members, yet one body" (1 Cor. 12:19–20). Earlier Paul suggests that diversity is part of God's plan and thus is God's desire (v. 18). There is divine intentionality behind the diversity of ecclesial "embodiment." Here Paul is speaking in the context of a discussion about spiritual gifts. Each person is gifted in a certain way, and all gifts are valuable. But later in the chapter Paul goes on to speak about honoring those who are less honorable or inferior, respecting those who are less respected, and so on. Rhetorically, the argument shifts from the church's giftedness to features of social standing or public perception. Diversity, then, can involve different things, but clearly it belongs in a discussion about ecclesial unity.

One could specify further by saying that body diversity and social-standing diversity are featured in Scripture as part of the church's unity. Homogeneity related to race/ethnicity, gender, and class is *not* part of an account of Christian unity. For this, we can turn to another Pauline passage: "There is no longer Jew or Greek, there is no longer slave or free, there is no longer male and female; for all of you are one in Christ Jesus" (Gal. 3:28). As remarkable as these words are by the apostle, sadly, the church has struggled up to the present day along these three specific stratifications. First, the Jewish-Greek divide mired the early church in tremendous conflict, leading to many types of tensions, as noted in Scripture itself, along with sundry accounts from early Christian history. These conflicts were largely cultural, but they had significant theological consequences, and they paved the way for a massive shift in terms of Christian identity (from an early Jewish sect to a predominantly Gentile religion that would eventually enjoy the favor of the empire).

As to the second matter, the slave-free dynamic was many things, but at the very least it was an economic arrangement in the New Testament era, speaking to class distinctions of varying kinds. For us today, class divisions prohibit Christian unity. We belong to a church tradition (Free Methodism) that felt the burden of this kind of ecclesial division at the time of its founding, given that the upward class mobility of American Protestantism generally and of American Methodism in particular during the mid-nineteenth century meant that even within church gatherings it became clear who was of means and who was not. The slave-free dynamic can also mean something quite particular in the United States. Those of us in this context who read this passage cannot help but relate it to the great blight upon American society: the formal institution of American chattel slavery and its heritage and ongoing influence through various practices, sensibilities, and habits within our culture. On this point, again sadly, the church on the whole has not had a resolute witness that consistently renounces dehumanizing and prejudice-perpetuating arrangements.

And finally, gender disparity and sexism continue to work against Christian unity. Women have typically comprised a majority in Christianity yet continue to be marginalized within the church in terms of their participation and roles in ecclesial structures. Even churches that openly promote women's full participation in ministry struggle with this challenge. Time and time again, women have been told by Christian men with power to "remain silent" and to look for other channels through which to contribute to the church's life, quite apart from the ways they may have been gifted and called. As such, the church has often struggled with and lost the service and witness of women who are made capable by God to serve the whole in particular ways.

In short, the call of Christian community is to work against a kind of uniformity of embodiment where everybody looks, thinks, and acts alike and values the same things. Such uniformity reifies divisions and social stratifications already reflected in a given context. When this happens, power arrangements and forms of marginalization set in. In opposition to this, Christians are called to welcome people's varied bodies and experiences into ecclesial fellowship. Such is a gesture of radical hospitality, to be sure; it can also be a prophetic denunciation of the wider societal structures and arrangements that segregate and marginalize human bodies from one another. What all of this means is that the church is called to be an alternative kind of community.

But what about the peculiar case of doctrinal uniformity? Is the church's unity based on a call to believe the same things in the same way? This matter is tricky and distinct from the previous concern. In the above point, people often *implicitly* divide on the basis of body and status-related similarities: "like tends to like" as people gather, make decisions, and live together over time.[2] But Christians (especially those who find themselves within the orbit of Protestant denominationalism) often *explicitly* divide on the basis of beliefs, possibly even many times over. In fact, beliefs are frequently understood by Christians as the gateway or foundation for proper practice and *not* vice versa. For example, when certain Protestants state that the marks of the "true church" are the proclamation of the gospel and the proper administration of the sacraments, in the background can stand a number of commitments related to what specifically constitutes "the gospel" and a "proper administration" of the sacraments. Nevertheless, when doctrinal debates ensue and ecclesial divisions take place as a result, what can be communicated is the idea that doctrinal agreement is to be sought. Through these developments, a uniformity of belief may be implied as a goal that serves church unity.

Practically, though, an account of these matters has to run deeper and be more nuanced than what appears on the surface. On the one hand, of course, at some level there has to be a sense of doctrinal definition and thus specification and demarcation. Peter's answer and confession in relation to Jesus's identity is pivotal: "You are the Messiah [Christ], the Son of the living God" (Matt. 16:16). In this Matthean account Jesus declares that on "this rock" (which we take to be Peter's confession) he will build his church (v. 18). Doctrines and beliefs matter for the sake of identity and tradition-negotiation. Yet on the other hand, doctrines are not simply propositional statements that require assent. They are not

2. For a challenging look into these kinds of processes, see Cleveland, *Disunity in Christ*.

typically formulated to be policing mechanisms to help determine who is "in" and "out" of ecclesial fellowship. If doctrines were to be chiefly used in such ways (and lamentably they often are), they would be reduced to roles that would take away from their main purpose within the church's life.

What then are doctrines, and what is their chief function within the church? Briefly, doctrines are accounts of the church's beliefs, formulations of the church's confession that help the church be faithful in its witness to the God of its worship. Of course, what it means to be faithful is a complex topic that can be understood in various ways. Some may take the term to imply a kind of allegiance that figuratively (and maybe even literally) implies "signing on the dotted line." We are inclined to think of faithfulness in a different way, in terms of the impact and significance of the church's witness within particular locations and situations. For example, to proclaim Jesus as "the Messiah [Christ], the Son of the living God" is a basic confession of Christianity, and efforts to secure, sustain, and elaborate this claim are typically seen as the proper domain of doctrine. And yet for the church to be faithful to this claim in first-century Palestine would require different gestures than ones associated with twenty-first-century America. What we are arguing is that doctrines are not simply statements or propositions but prompts that aim toward the perpetuation of a certain kind of life—a life in the Spirit, seeking conformity to Christ. We believe there is an ethical dimension to Christian doctrine, a formative aspect and not simply an informative one.[3] Since there are these aspects, doctrines as prompts toward faithfulness can in turn lead to narrative-attuning, improvisational, and varied performances of the Christian life.[4]

In short, the church is not called to a stagnant and artificial uniformity; quite the contrary, it is called to live into and embody a "sanctified diversity" in which questions related to bodies, class, and the character of faithful witness can be openly deliberated and negotiated. This may sound like a lofty, otherworldly goal, but "for God all things are possible" (Matt. 19:26).

---

3. For more on this point, see Hauerwas, "On Doctrine and Ethics."
4. We are here thinking of Wells, *Improvisation*.

The Church's Unity Is Grounded in the Trinity's Activity

If what the church is called to is not uniformity but a kind of unity that exists in diversity, then how is the latter possibility to be understood and lived out? The unity of the church, like all of the Niceno-Constantinopolitan marks, is not the church's achievement; otherwise the church could claim confidently that its unity is a feature of its own doing, a result of its concerted striving. But such an understanding would occasion human pride and dishonesty about human limits.

The church's unity is significant in part because it speaks to something that makes the church distinctive: it is a community grounded in something other than itself for its very existence and sought-after character. The claim of the church's unity is a confession, and it is a confession particularly of One beyond the church's life who sustains it to its very core. What we are saying is that the church's unity relies on and subsists in God's very life, a life that itself involves a unique account of unity and diversity.

How can the church's life be said to be grounded in the Trinity's life? How can the church's unity be sustained by and in God's unity? These are difficult questions, ones that have had a variety of answers and proposals over the years. With such a wide-ranging discussion, a number of legitimate concerns have presented themselves. On one end, there are proposals that lean positively to the idea that "the Trinity is our social program" (in the words of Nicholas Fedorov) or "social vision" (a qualification of Fedorov by Miroslav Volf).[5] While there are significant concerns to be registered all around with such a claim, these need not serve to entirely disqualify the analogous connection to be made. Worth noting here is the notion of perichoresis (Greek: *perichōrēsis*), which etymologically does not mean "dancing around" but rather "making space." The unity of the Trinity is perichoretic: the persons interpenetrate and are "personally interior to one another," such that distinction and unity apply within God's very life.[6] Within the economy, the point is registered repeatedly with turns of phrase from the Johannine Jesus, culminating in the claim "The Father and I are one" (John 10:30).

5. See Volf, "'The Trinity Is Our Social Program.'"
6. Volf, "'The Trinity Is Our Social Program,'" 409.

On another end, some scholars have shown caution in making these kinds of connections. One major concern is the case of projecting onto the triune life a social program or perspective already assumed and subsequently using the triune life as a way of justifying it. This process happens repeatedly in social trinitarianism and even with the language of perichoresis itself.[7] When such a process is given free rein, the veracity of theological speech is severely jeopardized: theologizing simply becomes a validating process for whatever happens to be the favored or customary perspective of the day.

We cannot press deeper into these discussions here, but we do wish to stress the importance of God's unity being *on display* in the economy of salvation and healing. Rather than a principle requiring abstract elaboration and extension, we take the Trinity's unity to be reflected within salvation history through the activity of this self-disclosing One. Once again, we come back to the Gospel of John. At the very start of this Gospel, we see allusions to the unity and diversity of the Godhead: "In the beginning was the Word, and the Word was with God, and the Word was God. He was in the beginning with God. All things came into being through him, and without him not one thing came into being" (John 1:1–3). Further epistemic claims speak to this unity and diversity: "No one has ever seen God. It is God the only Son, who is close to the Father's heart, who has made him known" (v. 18). Time and time again we see difference and unity working in tandem in the mission of the Son incarnate. After the healing of the lame man on the Sabbath, for instance, Jesus remarks, "Very truly, I tell you, the Son can do nothing on his own, but only what he sees the Father doing; for whatever the Father does, the Son does likewise" (5:19). At another point he remarks, "When you have lifted up the Son of Man, then you will realize that I am he, and that I do nothing on my own, but I speak these things as the Father instructed me" (8:28). Remarks like these show both an intimacy and a distinction between the Father and Son within the economy of salvation. And this unity in diversity is further perpetuated with the reference to the presence and work of the Holy Spirit. Early in the Gospel, John relates the words of the Baptist: "He whom God has sent speaks the words of God, for he gives the

7. For more on the point, see Kilby, "Perichoresis and Projection."

Spirit without measure. The Father loves the Son and has placed all things in his hands" (3:34–35). And of course, one finds later in the book the farewell discourse (chaps. 14–17), where the Spirit is spoken of prominently in conjunction with the activity of the Son and Father (see, for instance, 14:16, 26; 16:13–15).

This unity in diversity, then, is evident and sustained in salvation history, and it is this particular history that gives the notion a unique character. These particulars include specific actions and gestures that suggest a reorientation of the religious and cultural milieu of Jesus's day. Again taking the case of the Gospel of John, one sees Jesus purifying the temple, encountering the woman from Samaria (involving gender and ethnic dynamics), healing a royal official's son (involving class distinctions), performing a miracle on the Sabbath, and so on. In each of these cases, Jesus's conformity to the Father's will and his actions as the one who proclaims "I am" result in border-defying, alternative accounts of those who are called his flock. In fact, they are called to be "one flock," and he is to be their "one shepherd" (John 10:16).

Ecclesial Life That Is One through Its Engagement

The unity that exists in God's triune life and is evidenced in salvation history is a unity that is inviting and welcoming. It is an expansive unity awaiting further perichoretic activity, meaning further interpenetration or "making room." In a passage that has strong eucharistic undertones, Jesus remarks,

> Very truly, I tell you, unless you eat the flesh of the Son of Man and drink his blood, you have no life in you. Those who eat my flesh and drink my blood have eternal life, and I will raise them up on the last day; for my flesh is true food and my blood is true drink. Those who eat my flesh and drink my blood abide in me, and I in them. Just as the living Father sent me, and I live because of the Father, so whoever eats me will live because of me. (John 6:53–57)

This passage illustrates a kind of eucharistic hospitality, a process of making room before a table where people can gather around and abide in the Lord.

The Gospel of John expands on such interpenetrating imagery in chapter 15, the famous husbandry passage. Again, a unity of triune identity is affirmed yet simultaneously differentiated ("I am the true vine, and my Father is the vinegrower," v. 1), but now we have an address to the disciples, the community of the faithful, the one, true church: "Abide in me as I abide in you. Just as the branch cannot bear fruit by itself unless it abides in the vine, neither can you unless you abide in me. I am the vine, you are the branches. Those who abide in me and I in them bear much fruit, because apart from me you can do nothing" (vv. 4–5). The language of "abiding" sounds abstract until Jesus makes the call clear: "As the Father has loved me, so I have loved you; abide in my love. If you keep my commandments, you will abide in my love, just as I have kept my Father's commandments and abide in his love" (vv. 9–10). Several additional themes follow. The disciples are said to be friends of Jesus if they obey his commands (v. 14). They are to bear fruit and can rely on the Father on account of Jesus (v. 16). They will be persecuted by the world on account of the Son and the Father (vv. 18–25). And they are called to testify alongside the Spirit, who is sent from the Father at the request of the Son (vv. 26–27).

What are the implications of John 15 for the church and its unity? This passage of Scripture insists that the unity of the church—the one flock of the one Good Shepherd—can be cast not as something to be preserved but as something to be enacted by its very engagement and activity. Unity is a functional process more so than a status: unity is conditioned on obedience to Christ's commandments to love one another as Christ loved them. They are to bear fruit that will last. The Son's incarnation and the Spirit's coming both indicate actions by the one Trinity to restore and heal humanity. The church is called to live its life and serve its role within this revealed mission.

The church's unity, then, is a feature of both its discipleship and its call and so must be treated as a spiritual discipline that requires enactment but in a way that locates human agency within the revealed, active, and united life of the Trinity. Apart from this, the practice of ecclesial unity can easily morph into a segregated and policed uniformity, thereby compromising what is to be distinctive of Christian fellowship in a fallen and hurting world. The church's unity is to be constituted by its Spirit-led engagement and not in spite of it. Such is the shape of the Trinity's life with us, and it is to be analogously envisioned as reflective of the church's life as well.

THE CHURCH-SCRIPTURE ANALOGY

In the divine economy, the church's distinctive role as the chosen herald and agent of God's saving grace underwrites its uniqueness. The church is one of a kind. At the same time, as we noted above, outsiders often view the church as fragmented, not of "one heart and soul." For this reason, Paul encourages his readers to "make an effort to preserve the unity of the Spirit with the peace that ties you together" (Eph. 4:3 AT). A fractured body of Christ dulls the spiritual senses, making it difficult to discern the ways of God and live into God's calling to be a light to the nations (see Isa. 42:6; 49:6).

Similarly, the affirmation that Scripture is one book may simply acknowledge that the Bible is a one-of-a-kind book envisaged by both its two-Testament form and its formative function. Only the most hardened skeptic would dismiss the Bible as just another ancient anthology of disparate religious writings, bound together during its production without any special sense of its enduring effect. But Christians receive the Bible as canonical, trusting that the postbiblical process of selecting, collecting, and ordering Scripture into a final form is guarantor of this uniqueness. In fact, our use of the singular noun "Scripture" throughout this book intends to convey our belief in Scripture's singular specialness within the divine economy as the auxiliary of God's Spirit in inspiring various ecclesial practices of Christian formation.

In any case, the mark of the church's oneness is nicely captured in Acts by the characterization of a community that lives together in "one heart and soul" (4:32). It is not its uniformity of worship style or even its shared theological grammar and doctrines that form its communal solidarity; rather, it is its shared experience of the Spirit and distribution of its material goods so that no division exists between the haves and the have-nots within the congregation. Recognizing early on that its own diversity harbors within it the threat of division (6:1–8), the church of Acts is gathered together in its diversity under a common apostolic witness and with shared social practices (2:42). The result is a striking family resemblance among all its members.

The diversity of communions that congregate as the one global church is, in fact, mirrored by the diversity of witnesses found within Scripture. The concern of this chapter's discussion of Scripture's oneness, then, is much like the fractured church that practices it: Can Scripture's unified voice—the word of one, triune God—be sounded from a text as diverse as this one? More than any other settled claim of modern critical orthodoxy, the academy has established the Bible's seemingly intractable *disunity*, which threatens to subvert the church's claim of Scripture's theological coherence in communicating God's gospel. Scripture may be unique, but its literary and theological materials are hardly uniform.

Moreover, the reconstruction of Scripture's reception history, which demonstrates its textual multivalency, has had the effect of relativizing its meaning. Compounding this effect, the practices of modern criticism isolate and focus on textual fragments and the particular locations that produced them, which further frustrates any sense of a coherent and consistent message.

Our concern is not how Scripture's diverse parts came to be composed, canonized, or differently interpreted by its many readers but how Scripture in its canonical (and so indissoluble) form as a means of grace communicates a coherent word from our one and only God. The failure of a methodological consensus that can approach Scripture without fragmenting its admittedly diverse parts into a cacophony of witnesses only underscores the importance of the quest for Scripture's oneness.

A Biblical Analogy of Unity in Diversity (1 Cor. 12)

Our affirmation of Scripture's oneness is grounded in a pneumatology that considers Scripture's formation and its formative performances to be an achievement of the Holy Spirit. We believe the Spirit selected a diversity of authored texts and then sanctified the post-biblical phenomena that ordered these authored texts into a biblical canon, which the church then recognized as effective for mediating all of God's word to all of God's people for all time. We believe this same Spirit who led in the production of Scripture now also leads in its performances to cultivate the church's ongoing communion with its living Lord. No biblical analogy better illustrates this point than one we have already alluded to above: Paul's depiction of the Spirit's distribution of a diversity of spiritual charisms for the common good according to 1 Corinthians 12.

Canonization, like spiritual gifting, is a process of discernment that is regulated by the church's Spirit-enabled profession that "Jesus is Lord" (1 Cor. 12:3; see also Rom. 10:9). Paul is careful to contrast the congregation's reception of the Spirit, who alone generates the church's profession of faith, with other potential but fraudulent sources (1 Cor. 12:2; see also Phil. 2:11). The test of genuine faith is measured by its observable effect (see 1 Thess. 5:19–21): only the Spirit enables a congregation's perception of and thus public speech about what is true. Likewise, only the Spirit's charismatic presence could have prompted the church's recognition of which writings were truly apostolic in content and measurably formative in effect; only in this way were they received as such into the biblical canon.

Programmatic for our present discussion of Scripture's unity is Paul's larger point that no single charism is more important for the entire congregation's common good than any other (1 Cor. 12:4–11). While there is a diversity of gifts, ministries, and empowerments (ἐνέργημα, *energēma*; v. 6), they are each distributed and activated by the same Spirit, Lord, and God. Critically, this gifting process is the Spirit's achievement; the Spirit decides what gift to give and activate within every member of Christ's ecclesial body.

We would allow that this biblical depiction of the Spirit's performance in choosing, distributing, and animating spiritual gifts within the church is roughly analogous to the Spirit's performance in choosing, canonizing, and inspiring the church's Scripture. Following the logic of Paul's discussion in 1 Corinthians 12, the church's actions in forming its Scripture are not self-determined as though it has the authority to do so. Scripture is a charismatic gift to the confessing community, which receives and uses this gift in a manner that is utterly dependent upon the Spirit's presence and power.[8] As we said previously, this dependence is grounded in God's life and work.

Moreover, Paul's metaphor of the human body is recruited to commend the functional importance of diversity: A human body consists of many body parts, each of which has an important role to perform in a healthy human. Even as the variegated body parts of each individual *Homo sapiens* form an interdependent and orderly whole, the Spirit's gifting of the diverse body of Christ animates the indispensable ministry of every member (1 Cor. 12:22) in the proper care of the entire congregation (vv. 25–26). Here again, we see a kind of radical hospitality at work, now stemming from a sense of holistic necessity.

The salient issue for our purposes is that Paul's conception of a Spirit-forged unity in diversity is entirely functional. His point is neither that the church is one nor that its membership is many. Rather, the Spirit's revelatory presence among the many who profess Jesus as Lord purposes a salutary effect that benefits all (v. 7). In fact, the metric that tests the performance of any spiritual gift, whether it is received from the Holy Spirit or moved by a "dumb idol," is whether it benefits the entire congregation.

By analogy, if Scripture is perceived as a charismatic gift, then any claim for its unity must take account of its diverse but interdependent body parts. The implication that Paul here rejects a hierarchy of charisms may also imply that the church's reception of Scripture presumes the functional importance of each part that would issue in the rejection of any "canon within the canon" or of the inhospitable use of any Scripture that fractures the body of Christ rather than aggressively unites and heals it. Only then will the church's affirmation of Scripture's oneness witness to the Spirit's presence.

The Unity of Scripture: A Diversity of Proposals

Although the affirmation of Scripture's unity is settled orthodoxy in most Christian communions, the limits of what is meant by this theological agreement remain contested. Even our beginning students

8. See Webster, *Holy Scripture*, 58–63.

quickly realize that the Bible is a single book consisting of different literary genres, each written in response to all kinds of crises by different authors at different times to a diversity of congregations shaped by different moments and social locations over an extended period of time. These more immediate impressions are only deepened by close readings. For example, students learn that the first five biblical books are purposefully gathered together into a discrete collection, which Jesus calls "Law" (Torah). Their recognition of the evident diversity within this collected and singular whole becomes more nuanced through study: Whether defined linguistically, theologically, or historically, the canonical Torah relates its five parts together in an integral way that performs a foundational role and has a similar effect upon all its readers. At the same time, the goods of this one collection are not replicated by any other canonical collection. In fact, our students learn that the biblical whole is at the very least a collection of diverse collections, even if it is not immediately evident how this diversity plays well together. While the modern academy in its reception of Scripture routinely offers explanations of this seemingly intractable *disunity*, it has been much less forthcoming in proposing constructive models that enable the confessing church to affirm a scriptural *unity* within such evident diversity without devolving into unhelpful reductionisms.

Michael Legaspi's important intellectual narrative plots the decisive shift during the Enlightenment from the study of Scripture to what he calls the "textualization of the Bible," which corresponded to the rise of "biblical studies" in the academy.[9] While many properties characterize this profound change of direction, one note Legaspi sounds is especially important for our discussion of Scripture's unity: Scripture's referent shifted away from God—whose identity, forged by confession and worship, foregrounded the church's quest for theological understanding—and moved instead to historical events whose exigency, reconstructed by historical research and reason, provides the backdrop of reliable interpretation. The result was a critical fragmentation: Scripture was no longer read as a coherent witness to the

---

9. See broadly Legaspi, *Death of Scripture*.

divine economy but as an ancient library of diverse volumes, each shaped within different social locations by a diversity of historical contingencies and theological grammars. The triumph of disunity over unity produced—and continues to produce—atomistic readings of small bits and unrelated pieces of the Bible, sometimes resulting in an imbalanced myopia that inhospitably privileges one part of the biblical canon over other parts of its whole.

Nowhere does the problem of Scripture's diversity present itself more clearly than in the differences easily observed between its two Testaments. Some are content to keep each Testament at arm's length from the other. Popular perspectives of the independence of the Old Testament from the New Testament include variations of the so-called Marcionite heresy, in which the Old Testament is dismissed or neglected as an inferior revelation that lacks the clarity needed to function in forming the faith of its readers. For example, we often must correct our beginning Bible students who think that Israel's God is portrayed as wrathful and vindictive in the Old Testament and is now somehow displaced by the New Testament God, whose love and generosity are incarnate in Jesus—a distinction that cannot survive a close reading of Scripture itself. We simply open the Letter to the Hebrews, whose theology of Scripture as God's "living and active" word (4:12) includes Israel's God speaking through the Old Testament prophets (1:5–13; 2:11–13; 3:7–11) and the New Testament apostles (2:3–4) simultaneously!

We detect this same reductionism, however, in modern critical approaches that read the Old Testament and New Testament as historical reflections of independent eras of religious sentiment. In this case, the Old Testament and New Testament constitute discrete histories of religion; their unity is not only impossible to construct but unnecessary to seek. In fact, the historian's recovery of the Bible's diverse tracks from the ancient past—and so the defeat of the church's affirmation of the Bible's unity—became the goal of an academic approach to biblical studies. Even the biblical theology movement, mostly sponsored by church-related institutions, reads Scripture as a chorus of biblical theologies, each of which vocalizes God's word in a different key.

Of course, the rich diversity of theologies we find in Scripture was an accepted characteristic of the biblical canon from its very origin.

After all, Irenaeus, who first conceived of the church's two-Testament Scripture, noted that heresy is often the result of reducing the Bible's multivalency to a single voice—in Marcion's case, for example, a Pauline voice without the correcting effect of other apostolic witnesses. The constructive use of Scripture's own diversity, then, can provide an apparatus of checks and balances that keeps biblical interpretation on target.

More significant than proposals that accept criticism's fragmentation of Scripture as a new orthodoxy are proposals seeking an overarching unity that overcomes Scripture's diversity in constructive, compelling ways. Trading on a trinitarian conception of the church's oneness marked by God's hospitality toward and engagement with "the other," current approaches seeking Scripture's unity share a common feature: cultivating hospitable relationships between Scripture's disparate parts. Such an approach is in keeping with what we have noted above.

Most of those seeking such a strategy find and in fact demand a hermeneutical key for doing so within Scripture itself. Perhaps the most prominent schemas of unity are conceptually programmatic but rather vague around the edges. Their purpose is to provide readers with a wide-angle lens that helps them navigate through the thicket of diverse texts in a way that excludes none. For example, one might read Scripture as a continuous story with a beginning, middle, and end. From the perspective of a story's reader, Scripture begins with two interpenetrating episodes of creation: God first creates earth, then Israel, through whom the Creator promises to bless all the families of the earth. The Old Testament narrative continues by recounting Israel's sojourn with its covenant-keeping God, which climaxes in the New Testament's gospel narrative of God's Messiah, Jesus, the denouement of which is told in Acts and the New Testament letters. Scripture's story finds its rousing conclusion in Revelation's vision of the apocalypse of a new creation inhabited by the triune God and by God's people, who experience the full measure of God's promised salvation.

Scripture's story, most often of creation's redemption, is sometimes plotted as a chronology of events, with each event introducing a core theme that unfolds in an organic way. From this angle the Old

Testament history of Israel provides readers with a set of conceptual categories that the New Testament story of Jesus and the church takes over and completes. Those who follow this schema of unity, especially Protestants, tend to read Scripture from left to right and so place a premium on the events that launch the story in Genesis 1–4. G. K. Beale's recent contribution is the exception. He reads this same story line from right to left, arguing that Scripture's narrative movement is eschatological and thus that the *telos* of Israel's history, of Jesus's life, and of the apostolic mission of the church is new creation—a story line of fulfillment from beginning to end, shaped by a prior reading of Scripture's concluding chapter in the Apocalypse.[10] The advantage of Beale's schema is that it offers a response to the oft-heard criticism that most suggestions of Scripture's unifying center must be grounded in the New Testament (and, we would contend, in a Pauline "canon within the canon"). Indeed, it is the Old Testament's eschatological vision of newness (creation, covenant) that "unfolds" allusively in the New Testament in a way that unifies the whole.

The variety of biblical episodes that mark the story's beginning (e.g., creation, covenant, exodus, law-giving, wilderness, land, and so on) are often recast as biblical types or theological patterns of divine activity that are repeated throughout Scripture in a way that unifies old with new. Similarly, others trade on Jesus's comment in the Sermon on the Mount when he tells his disciples—against the accusations of his opponents—that he has come to fulfill Israel's scripture rather than to abolish it (see Matt. 5:17–18; Luke 24:44–47). On this basis, then, the two Testaments are envisaged as a dialogue between prophets and apostles: the promises of the prophets (Old Testament) are considered fulfilled by apostolic witness (New Testament). Matthew 1 may even function as a canonical seam in this regard: God's promises to the people of Abraham and David are faithfully realized by the birth of Immanuel.

Our canonical approach to Scripture commends the aesthetic excellence of its final shape. One important feature of this aesthetic is the purposeful sequence of its canonical collections, a sequence that forms working relationships, which not only reflect an overarching

---

10. Beale, *New Testament Biblical Theology*.

"canon logic" that binds Scripture together as a coherent whole but also maximize the communicative effectiveness of Scripture's witness to God's word. Broadly speaking, the fivefold Pentateuch's role in the Old Testament performs a role similar to that of the fourfold Gospel: both provide the theological ground on which their respective Testaments are constructed. The historical narrative of Israel's rise and fall in the promised land performs a similar role to Acts in the New. Likewise, the instruction of Old Testament Wisdom is not unlike the role performed by the New Testament letters. Both in temper and in topic, the similarity between the prophetic books and the Apocalypse, which the prophet introduces as "words of the prophecy" (Rev. 1:3), is self-evident. This correlation between the final form of the two canonical Testaments envisages an aesthetical or rhetorical unity, which we think should frame any reading strategy of Scripture as a whole.

Another kind of literary unity focuses on the intertextuality between New Testament and Old.[11] The formation of the biblical canon produces a new textual context in which an author's scriptural quotations and allusions and the echoes reverberating between appointed lessons create a dialogue between texts within Scripture and thereby witness to a unified word from God. Richard Hays concludes that such a dialogue extends to readers and commissions them to retell the gospel story in fresh ways for their brave new world.[12]

The long-standing quest for Scripture's internal unifying theme still persists. Most fail to find this quest convincing; the discontinuities we find within Scripture are too great a barrier to overcome. The suggested center of Scripture is either too broad to account for its complexity (e.g., a divine attribute such as God's mercy) or too narrow to include this same complexity (e.g., a particular event from Jesus's life such as his exemplary life or messianic death). If the quest were to move forward, we would need to agree on a set of guiding criteria, of which there are three that come immediately to mind: (1) Scripture itself should be the source of its own unifying center. (2) The scope of Scripture's center should unify both Old Testament

---

11. For more on the topic, see Wall, "Intertextuality, Biblical."
12. Hays, *Echoes of Scripture in the Gospels*, 366.

and New Testament. That is, one could not propose a unifying center of the New Testament while presuming that it would do the same heavy lifting for the Old Testament or vice versa. This must be a biblical, not a testamental, norm. (3) Finally, each demonstration of a unifying center should evince its own distinctive contribution to a fully biblical conception; it should not borrow from or merely quote from an antecedent tradition as though it were its own.

Perhaps the strongest case for this kind of scriptural unity is made by our colleague Eugene Lemcio, who has found evidence of what he calls a "unifying kerygma" in both Old Testament and New Testament and in every canonical collection of each.[13] Our concern with Lemcio's proposal is that the particular elements of his conception of "gospel" are too vague to account for the distinctive theological contribution of the different biblical witnesses that form and inform the entire revelatory word.

Our Proposal: The Apostolic Rule of Faith and the Simultaneity of Scripture

We are convinced that Jesus's commissioning of his apostles provides the hermeneutical key that underwrites the church's affirmation of Scripture's unity. According to Luke's Gospel (24:44–48), Jesus commissions his apostles to be witnesses of a messianic reading of Israel's tripartite Scripture. Jesus does not teach a unifying theme that pulls Scripture's disparate parts together but a unifying hermeneutic: an interpretive rubric external to the biblical text itself, unifying the different parts of Scripture ("the law of Moses, the prophets, and

13. See Lemcio, "Unifying Kerygma of the New Testament"; and "Unifying Kerygma of the New Testament (II)." These were combined and expanded in an appendix to his *The Past of Jesus in the Gospels*. Departing from C. H. Dodd's attempt to assemble a kerygma from the New Testament and avoiding James D. G. Dunn's effort to abstract a kerygma from it, Lemcio claims to have detected a version of God's gospel from within Scripture, whose theo-centric nature is as follows (regardless of sequence): (1) God who promises to bless (2) sent (the Gospels) or (3) raised Jesus. (4) A response (receiving, repentance, faith, obedience) (5) toward God (6) brings the faithful promised benefits/blessings (variously described). Although the titles of Lemcio's studies locate this unifying center in the New Testament, his second study extends it to the Old Testament as well.

the psalms"), and doing so in a way that illumines God's redemptive plan ("repentance and forgiveness of sins").

We commend two moves based on what we take as the priority of Jesus's way of unifying Scripture. First, the combination of "understanding" (συνίημι, *syniēmi*) about "what is written" (γέγραπται, *gegraptai*) implies that Jesus "opened their minds to understand the scriptures" (v. 45) by teaching the apostles about himself. For members of an apostolic community, Jesus is Scripture's singular referent. He plainly says that what is written in Israel's scripture is "about me" (v. 44); Scripture's communicative intention targets his messianic life and its redemptive effect: "repentance and forgiveness of sins."

This intellectual awareness of Scripture's coherence is possible only among those who agree with the apostles' witness while Jesus "was still with [them]" (v. 44) and with the instruction they subsequently received from the risen Jesus (see Acts 1:3–8)—namely, that what is written in Scripture is actually about him. Jesus's instruction of his apostles forms and frames a way of bringing to focus all the parts of Scripture rather than the retrieval of one unifying theme found within Scripture. What is essential in any description of Scripture's unity is not the reader's preoccupation with its diversity, especially as modern criticism determines and has now described it, but its unity with God in the flesh, the living Christ. In this sense, the simultaneity of the various parts of Scripture is not undone and left without a clear and coherent message for today's readers, because its single subject matter is divine and not bound to change because of time or place.[14]

Second, Luke's redaction of Jesus's Great Commission—that his apostles announce God's salvation to the nations "in his name" (24:47)—includes this christological hermeneutics of Scripture. Significantly, the antecedent of "these things" (ταῦτα, *tauta*) in Jesus's

14. See Levenson, "Eighth Principle of Judaism," 213. If God's intended meaning is posited in the whole of the church's Scripture, the simultaneity of its Old and New Testaments conveys a sense that there is really no perceived chasm between what the old "meant" in Israel's past and what the new now "means" in the church's present. The text received and a text that reinterprets it for theological understanding are equally valued texts in the dynamic process that seeks to hear and then submit to the word of the Lord God Almighty—a word that Christians believe is incarnate in God's Son, Jesus of Nazareth, and is made ever new by God's Spirit.

command to "witness to these things" (v. 48) plausibly presumes that the community's proclamation of the gospel includes a way of reading Scripture that agrees with the risen Jesus's instruction of his apostles. Sharply put, the church's mission in the world presumes that the use of "what is written" in Scripture is made coherent by a normative way of interpreting what is written by the apostles who learned from the risen Jesus.

A reading of Scripture that guarantees the clarity and coherence of Scripture's redemptive message to all nations is what Irenaeus proposed as the "Rule of Faith," which the church received from the apostles, who learned it from their witness of and instruction from the historical Jesus, the incarnate Son. Even before Irenaeus, 2 Timothy instructs a congregation of readers to "accurately handle [ὀρθοτομέω, orthotomeō; literally, "cut a straight or accurate line"] the word of truth" (2:15 AT). While such close attention to this word surely includes close linguistic analysis that accurately assesses what the biblical text actually says, every faithful reader's endgame is to understand a sacred text as the communicative medium of God's word that issues in practical wisdom and forms a congregation's common life and global mission.[15]

Distinct from but in cooperation with the standard rules of modern biblical criticism, the simultaneity of this Rule of Faith received from the Lord's apostles, however it is articulated, presumes to continually constrain what an interpreter may or may not retrieve from a canonical text for the community's theological and moral instruction. This interpretive strategy is predicated on Jesus's insistence that the substance of what was written in Scripture in the past is timeless and made ever relevant by its "accurate handling." Scripture is by nature and practice a hermeneutical book. That is, Scripture requires both a critical reading of what it literally says, which may expose its diversity and even discontinuity, and a theological reading of what it teaches the faithful about the gospel of Messiah Jesus. The hermeneutical rubric by which we

15. I have elaborated this understanding of the apostolic Rule of Faith in a number of publications. My experimental use of it as an interpretive rubric is found in Wall, 1 & 2 Timothy and Titus; see also the more theological piece "Rule of Faith in Theological Hermeneutics."

might accomplish the latter task, which also exposes Scripture's unity, is supplied by the Rule of Faith.

We admit that the construction of any version apropos of this apostolic Rule, whether by Irenaeus or by us, involves a circularity that draws its working grammar of theological agreements from Scripture in order to read Scripture coherently. We insist, however, that a faithful reader's self-critical employment of this interpretive rubric will also attend to the diversity of Scripture's literal meaning before engaging in its Rule-based figural reading, thereby to bring unity to all Scripture. Further, there should be consistent application of this same Rule across the diverse witnesses that comprise the entire biblical canon.

Concluding Thoughts

How then does the analogy of the church's unity help us in understanding Scripture's unity? We have noted that unity is not uniformity: there can be unity amid diversity. In fact, the manner in which God works involves precisely such an interplay of unity and diversity. This may be hard for some to accommodate, given their views and expectations as to what unity entails. Our aim has been to show that unity and diversity work together because they are fundamental to God's activity in the world. Diversity here is not a threat to unity; rather, it is very much constitutive of it. In this sense, unity is not a status or a state; it is a functional dynamic, a way of subsisting. This understanding serves the purpose of elaborating both the church and Scripture.

The church as the body of Christ lives into this unity through its conformity to the character of Christ through the power of the Holy Spirit. As segregated as church life can be, we believe that this "alternative community" is one in which people of all walks of life can contribute to the whole as distinct members of one body. Analogously, it is very possible to fracture the Bible as it is being engaged. This fracturing is something that is perpetuated by the patterns and methods of the academy. And yet, each canonical voice has its part; these voices too can be thought of as members of the "canonical body" of writing that is Scripture, and each voice has a role to play as Scripture collectively bears witness to the living Christ. Such is the providential makeup of these specific formations.

The tendency toward division, whether manifested in terms of ecclesial segregations of various kinds or in terms of a biblical "canon within the canon," is to be actively resisted. Within this temptation lies a kind of inhospitality driven by any number of factors, including fear, groupthink, the desire for respectability, and so on. But ultimately we have stressed that the unity that is to be at work within the church and in the reading practices of Scripture is enabled and driven by the Spirit's work; it is not a human achievement per se. We sense that the kinds of divisions we see so blatantly in effect in church life, as well as in the ways people read and think through Scripture, grieve the Spirit very much. The path forward in all of this is to champion and embody an ethos in which "living in the Spirit" and "reading in the Spirit" are connected. How? Via a vibrant spirituality in which the church and Scripture are manifest as means of grace through which God the Spirit works to sustain, over time and within history, a gospel witness to the incarnate, crucified, resurrected, and ascended Son.

Holiness

We continue our exploration of the marks by looking at how the church and Scripture can be cast as "holy." For generations, Scripture has often been called "the Holy Bible" or "Sacred Writ," which may have had the long-term effect among some constituencies of divinizing it. At the same time, given the many profane details that have come to light about ecclesial life generally, it has been increasingly difficult to see the church as holy. And yet amid these polarities one senses the creative tension and possibility for generative recalibration. If the church can be critically and constructively thought of as holy, the claim that Scripture too is holy may be more chastened and thus helpful. At work in this is the need to rethink the notion of holiness altogether, which is a significant feat all its own in our skeptical age.

PRACTICAL AND DOGMATIC CONSIDERATIONS

One of the worst recent happenings in the church's life has been the child-abuse scandal, which has embroiled the Roman Catholic Church in particular. Child abuse is undoubtedly one of contemporary society's most offensive crimes, given the powerlessness, innocence, and fragility of children and the impact their early experiences

can have for the duration of their lifetimes. To be sure, the toll is
heavy for the abused. It is also heavy for the church as a whole, both
internally and externally. Internally, it may be difficult to establish
forgiveness and reconciliation within the church's life given just how
offensive this crime is. Externally, if an issue could convince the onlooking world of the hypocrisy of the church, surely it would be
this one. The church's divisions are egregiously evident, but its sins
irredeemably offensive, thereby undermining the confession of the
church's sanctity or holiness and (again) the appeal of this form of
human community.

Holiness is a difficult topic to broach, not simply because of scan-
dals such as this one, but also because of deeply held commitments
of an anthropological and soteriological (that is, salvation-related)
kind. These commitments sometimes favor the definition of holiness that emphasizes separation more so than other views that stress
gospel wholeness, fullness, and even happiness. For the two of us,
who teach at a Methodist institution, the topic hits especially close
to home. Methodism's origins are as a renewal movement, and one
of its long-standing charisms to the wider Christian church has been
its emphasis on the possibility of holiness in this life. Common terms
here are "sanctification" and even "Christian perfection." Yet students regularly appear in our classrooms with faulty assumptions and
views surrounding the notion.[1] One popular view is that holiness is
not possible in this lifetime. Students tend to say this because of an
anthropological commitment they see and hear repeatedly in their
local churches that is registered via many different biblical passages,
including Romans 3:23 ("All have sinned and fall short of the glory
of God"). This commitment is that we are and always will be sinners
in this life. Implications of this commitment include the following:
Humans are born in sin, and their status persists as such. We are
"*sinners* saved by grace"; with this emphasis, we can never possibly
be saints. And if such is the case with individuals, the view is only
exacerbated with collectives: A community cannot possibly be holy
if it is made up of sinners; who they are collectively will only reflect

---

1. For a helpful account of many different "hurdles to holiness," see Van De Walle,
Rethinking Holiness, 24–27.

(perhaps even in more severe form) who they are individually. The conclusion, then, is that the church cannot be holy but is fallen and sinful and thus needs to confess and be forgiven.

And yet the tradition of the church and even the pages of Scripture affirm a more expansive vision. Early in Paul's First Epistle to the Corinthians he speaks to the possibility of holiness in this life: "To the church of God that is in Corinth, to those who are sanctified in Christ Jesus, called to be saints" (1:2). But as readers of this letter know, the Corinthian church is saddled by all kinds of sin and corruption. Was Paul being polite or disingenuous by using this language, or could there be more to the claim of the church's sanctity than what appears at first blush? We will pursue the latter line of questioning in roughly the same fashion as the previous chapter, moving from apophatic claims to theo-logical confession that is missional in orientation.

We Are Not Created to Be Sinners

An assumption at work for some of our students, including those cited above and many others, is that holiness is an otherworldly reality, one that characterizes a heavenly (and not an earthly) situation. Coupled with this is the belief that God is holy and none other. Of course, there is some truth to all of this. One of the hopes of Christians regarding the afterlife is that struggle, pain, and sin will not hold their power in the way they do now. And it is true that God is transcendent and unlike anything or anyone else. But what about our lives here and now?

In speaking of how "reality works," Christians tend to operate out of networks of assumptions and logics that they typically "pick up" rather than delve into for debate, exploration, and possible readjustment.[2] If one were to question these networks, it would be hard work that involves asking deep questions about the significance of life and God's purposes as well as the manner in which we interpret and face our experiences and circumstances. But such work is important because, without it, a number of facets of Christian existence

2. I (Castelo) speak of this phenomenon more extensively in "Spirit, Creaturehood and Sanctification."

would be ignored, and such a loss would be detrimental not simply to individuals but also to the church as a whole.

So where shall we begin in the probing of these networks? Here is one question to explore: What is the connection between being creatures and being holy? The assumption pointed to above suggests that being human means being profane or unholy. For some Christians, there is no connection between humanness and holiness because only God is truly and properly holy, and so, by definition, nothing and no one else could be. If this is true, then humans—simply by being humans—cannot be holy. The point is further reinforced with the widely held sensibility that it is improper for us to refer to others or to ourselves as holy since the claim would be a sign of human self-absorption and maybe even idolatry. Exhibit A in support of this point would be the holier-than-thou crowd who think they are on a higher plane of existence than everyone else because of their self-proclaimed status as "holy Christians." These people can be judgmental and legalistic while failing to show the compassion and love of Jesus to their neighbors. Given all these pitfalls, most skeptics assume that it is better to avoid the language of holiness altogether. We may be able to refer to ourselves as loving, compassionate, merciful, and just—characteristics that we in fact do employ to think and talk about God—but holiness seems to be in a category all its own, something distinctive of God and God alone.

But let's take a step back. Humans are created by a holy God, and humans are created in the image and likeness of God (Gen. 1:26–27). If one looks to the history of Christian reflection, many possibilities present themselves in terms of specifying what the image is, but we wish to focus right now on the point that if humans are created in God's image, then God's creative activity is not simply the making of a distinct and separate other (God's *image and likeness*) but also the impartation and engagement of God's very self (*God's* image and likeness). When God created humans, God shared something about Godself that in turn is reflected in humans themselves. Therefore, even though it is quite remarkable that *any* language for God is possible (as apophatic theology contends, given that no language can really do justice to who God is), its foundation is precisely in this connectedness and relatedness implied by God's work of creating.

Humans can and do believe that human mercy is like God's mercy and that human love is like God's love because of what they come to believe of themselves and God through their experience of God's self-revelation. Truthful God-talk, then, is based on and funded by the relatedness at work in God's creative activity. If this makes possible the use of themes like mercy and love for the God-human interface, then why not also holiness?

Sometimes people object that holiness should be in a class of its own because it can be defined as "anti-sin," and humans have a connection to sin that God does not have. But in the same way, God's love and God's mercy can also be understood as "anti-sin," and humans often struggle mightily to be loving and merciful, against their sinful tendencies. Furthermore, we as Christians believe that, in Christ, God has confronted sin and has proved to be victorious over it. Taking all of this into account, there is no reason why holiness should be drastically different from these other markers. Humans struggle with living into the character and call that God has placed on them, but possibilities exist to do so since humans are God's creatures, created in God's image, and empowered by God's presence. Therefore humans are holy and can live in holiness because they are creatures created by a holy God, in a holy way, and for holy ends.

Notice, though, the implications of the above logic: If God's character is imparted to humans in the way God creates them, and if human sin does not prohibit us from making connections between God and ourselves in our thought and speech, then humans can be spoken of as holy *even within* the conditions of sinfulness. The goal here is not to blur distinctions between sin and holiness but to problematize a spectrum of extremes. In many portrayals, humans are depicted as utterly deplorable this side of the fall, whereas God is understood to be holy as no other (thus making holiness a quality associated with God's transcendence). The disadvantage of this casting of extremes between God and humans is that it fails to account for the creational logic outlined above; yet this logic, we argue, is fundamental to our understanding of who God is, how God works, and who we are as humans.

Let's extend this creational logic further. The Christian God did not create humans as sinners, nor did God create humans to become sinners. Sin, in other words, is not part of our God-intended essence and constitution as creatures. Sin is anti-creation and therefore anti-life, and in this way it can be understood as anti-holiness and anti-God. The impact of sin in the world and in our lives is tremendous, no doubt: many of the articulations highlighted above are helpful in reminding us of this point, given that it is so easy to sidestep or mini-mize the ongoing impact of sin (which itself is a sign of sinfulness!). And yet, after the fall, humans do not cease to be God's creatures. Despite collective and personal sin, we believe that the image of God persists within humans in some fashion. Why? First and foremost, because God repeatedly does not give up on humans specifically or on creation generally. God shows that creation is worth saving because it is God's. We see this time and time again in the biblical narrative, all the way back, one could say, to Noah and even to the garden of Eden itself. God is in the business of restoring and healing God's creation, not destroying and doing away with it. Is human sin offensive and destructive? Absolutely. But humans have an inherent dignity that is not lost after the fall. Their inherent dignity is based on the confes-sion that they are God's creatures, created in God's image, and worth saving by God's very self.

At stake in these remarks, then, are basic considerations related to what can be called a theological anthropology. Just as we have been asking of Scripture the ontological and teleological questions, we can also ask these questions of humans: What are humans, and what is their purpose? In short, the answer we would give is that humans are God's creatures who are created to worship and commune with God. On both scores, the language of holiness can be used. As creatures of God and bearing God's image, humans are created as holy: this is the basis of their dignity and worth. Furthermore, as creatures created to worship and commune with God, humans are created for holiness: that is their call and end.

Both this identity and this call are extended within the life of the church, which is the community of God's creatures actively seeking conformity and fellowship with the triune God. First Peter alludes to both aspects as the author remarks to his readers, "You are a chosen race, a royal priesthood, a holy nation, God's own people, in order that you may proclaim the mighty acts of him who called you out of darkness into his marvelous light" (2:9). The church is holy in that it is God's and no other's. God brought the church to be through Jesus's call and command: "Follow me." In turn, the church is called to proclaim the powerful acts of God, to live in active fellowship and conformity with the God of its worship. As Van De Walle extensively remarks, "The church's holiness, like the holiness of all created things, is never its own by nature. While the church's holiness is real, it is not self-constituted, self-sustained, or grounded in itself or its actions. Rather, the holiness of the church, like the holiness of any created thing, is a derived holiness,"[3] based on God's self and extended in God's acts. Through its life, the church can show another way to exist communally—a way of life that is seeking conformity to God's will.

However, as we noted at the beginning of this chapter, the church all too often does otherwise. The church is not called to be a sinful fellowship, but it often shows itself to be so. The church lives within the complexity that its individual participants live in, as creaturely entities constituted and called to be holy yet actively leading lives of corruption and profanity. The church in particular, like humans in general, lives in an ongoing state of active self-contradiction. Its only hope is precisely the God of its confession and worship.

The Church's Holiness Is the Triune God's Holiness

The gap created by sin is simply too vast for humans to bridge. We cannot "will our way" out of the self-contradiction that is at work in our individual and collective lives. For the language of holiness to be operative within such conditions, the ongoing activity of a holy God is needed. Put another way, "The church is holy not because of what it does or how it appears on the outside but because of its special relationship to the triune God."[4] For more on this, we turn to the economic manifestation of this triune God, that is, to the manifestation of God within our history and our world.

3. Van De Walle, *Rethinking Holiness*, 133.
4. Van De Walle, *Rethinking Holiness*, 140. For more on this point, see Goroncy, "The Elusiveness, Loss and Cruciality of Recovered Holiness."

To begin, in Christ we see "the Holy One of Israel" in our midst, God in the flesh. Given the wide expanse between Creator and creature, it may seem easier to focus on one or another end of this relationship, which is often what happens when scholars think of a "high" or "low" Christology. But part of the challenge of the incarnation is to think paradoxically and to hold the tension evidently at work within the confession that God has appeared in human likeness. A passage from the Epistle to the Hebrews is especially important here. The writer states, "For we do not have a high priest who is unable to sympathize with our weaknesses, but we have one who in every respect has been tested [tempted] as we are, yet without sin" (4:15). Given that sin is anti-creation because it is anti-God, the last part of this phrase ("yet without sin") makes very good sense. Furthermore, the confession of Christ's temptation or testing may run counter to certain theological accounts of anthropology, but these may be softened by the confession of Christ's virgin birth. With remarks such as these, one may sense an effort to make the incarnation of Christ "safe" from the perceived dangers of all that can be implied by the incarnation itself—of the holy God of Israel tabernacling among us who live within a fallen state. Our inclination as doctors of the church is to press rather than soften the paradox at work in this passage.

Briefly, we are inclined to take seriously the claim that Jesus's flesh was genuinely human flesh *this side* of the fall—that is, human existence as we presently understand and experience it.[5] As Karl Barth exhorts, "There must be no weakening or obscuring of the saving truth that the nature which God assumed in Christ is identical with our nature as we see it in the light of the Fall. If it were otherwise, how could Christ be really like us?"[6] Additionally, we are not disposed to frame the virgin birth strictly as a mechanism to preserve the point that Jesus was "without sin." We believe the virgin birth functions otherwise—namely, to suggest the truly miraculous nature of the event that One of the Trinity became human flesh. In short, we believe this passage from Hebrews makes the point that Christ

5. Thomas F. Torrance's reflections are especially helpful on this score; see his work *Incarnation*, 61–62.
6. Barth, *Church Dogmatics*, I/2, 153. We may not go as far as Barth does in his casting of fallen human nature, but we nevertheless agree with the quoted point above.

was genuinely human in broken and fallen conditions, yet he lived the kind of life that is most human and faithful, which is one in consistent conformity to the Father's will.

There is another point to account for in the above passage: a feature of Christ's high-priestly character is that he was in every way "tested" or "tempted" as we are. This confession dovetails nicely with another feature of the incarnation that has come through at various stages of the church's reflective life—namely, the claim that what is unassumed is unhealed. This commitment is sometimes cast as a patristic soteriological principle because it is prominent among several major church figures.[7] What this confession shows is that the manner in which the triune God bridged the gap between humans and their Creator was strategic: God's taking up of human flesh in post-fall conditions means that those of us who live within these conditions have a genuine Savior who is in solidarity with us. The famous logic of Athanasius nicely fits here: God took up human flesh so that we could become like God.[8]

This Athanasian principle holds in another domain of reflection on the economic work of the triune God: pneumatology. During the interim period between the Councils of Nicaea (325) and Constantinople (381), a flurry of activity surrounded the identity and work of the Holy Spirit. Athanasius himself, in a collection of letters typically titled *Letters to Serapion*, countered a group known as the "Spirit-fighters"—a sobriquet given to them for their objection to the Spirit's divinity. Athanasius is quite firm on the point: The Holy Spirit is God, and this because the Spirit is the agent of sanctification, the One who makes the Christian community holy.[9] The Holy Spirit certainly has a creational role (this, after all, is the "Spirit of life"), but the point pressed here by Athanasius is that the Spirit makes us holy—that is, the Spirit heals us, restores us, and transforms us. The blight of sin is significant, to be sure, but the Spirit's work of healing and sanctifying is such that God brings it forth within our very selves.

7. Origen, Athanasius, and the Cappadocians are some who are associated with this principle. See especially Gregory of Nazianzus, *Epistle 101*. Of course, what is particularly at stake when the principle is affirmed varies from case to case.

8. Athanasius, *On the Incarnation* 54.

9. See broadly Athanasius, *Letters to Serapion* 1.22.3–1.24.4.

The work of creation and the work of sanctification, then, are two important inflections to keep in mind within an account of the fallen state that currently mars the creation. These inflections are not strictly historical events but are ongoing dynamics: Humans are holy creatures, created by a holy God, living in and perpetuating a state of fallenness. Yet a way through that fallenness unto a glorious shape of holiness is provided presently by the triune God, as accented in the ongoing work of Christ and the Spirit. Therefore, the picture of humanity stemming from this depiction is quite complex. It will not do to simply use labels such as "sinners" or "saints," nor is there a practical need to place people in one or the other category, given the conflict-laden histories and experiences of all people. Rather, there are at least three interstices to account for when speaking of those who are "in Christ": creatures, sinners, saints. The first reflects divine agency; the second, human agency; and the third, a sophisticated synergy that involves both divine and human agency in their respective and appropriate functioning. It is to this last point that we presently turn.

The Call to Be a Holy People

The church's life works along these points: The church is constituted by the work of the triune God; as a people the church regularly fails and commits sin; and the church is called to be a community of saints. What often plagues the church in its habitation of these interstices is its collective speech when compared to its collective life. In this, the holiness of the church and (in the eyes of an onlooking world) the holiness of God are compromised. "Hallowed be your name" is an early plea for sanctification in the Lord's Prayer, which is appropriate since the church is all too often about the business of profaning God's name and God's call upon the church. For many, the church's confession of holiness can itself be an act of self-profaning in that it would be self-indicting.

So what to do? How can the language of holiness be claimed as a mark of ecclesial identity? One important step is to strongly align it with honest and nuanced self-evaluation. On this point, many of the above-mentioned patterns of Christian speech are spot-on: the refusal to claim holiness can be a gesture of honest self-evaluation in light of our standing and living before a holy God, the One who is like no other. At the same time—and not in any way to dismiss the importance of the previous point—a nuance should be preserved: namely, that the creature has been dignified by the work of the triune God in the act of the incarnation. Here the holy work of creation is reaffirmed because of the pathway made available toward new creation. Self-evaluation that is attentive not only to human realities and limits (recognizing that we are not God and are currently broken and in need of God's help) but also to human dignity (observing the claim that we are God's creatures and that God does not give up on us because we are God's) is crucial in reworking the language of holiness for its contemporary appropriation.

But beyond these points, something more is needed with regard to a vision for holiness in this life. What is needed is a vision for how to embody it, how to enact it. In other words, what is needed is an account of how to obey Jesus's command to "be perfect, . . . as your heavenly Father is perfect" (Matt. 5:48). Although space prohibits an adequate presentation, one incident from the biblical narrative concerning what "ecclesial holiness" could look like is particularly instructive.

John 13 is a chapter in John's Gospel that has no correspondences with the Synoptic Gospels. Whereas in the Synoptics the focus of Jesus's last evening with his disciples is on the Passover meal, for the Gospel of John, the focus is very much on another act: Jesus washing the feet of his disciples. From all accounts, this was quite a remarkable act, a pivotal moment in the Son's condescension to the human condition, and an act of radical servitude.[10] Notice that this is an embodied form of ministry: Jesus's hands touching, washing, cleaning, and purifying his disciples' feet. But there are other layers to this event as well. In both the Jewish and the Greco-Roman contexts of Jesus's day, the washing of one's feet was a practical necessity, but it also carried with it class distinctions since it was usually the work of slaves.[11] And yet in this scene, Jesus washes his disciples' feet,

---

10. For more on the significance of this act within the confines of the ancient world, see Thomas, *Footwashing in John 13*; also see generally his chapter "Footwashing within the Context of the Lord's Supper."

11. Thomas, *Footwashing in John 13*, 42, 56.

a scandalous act that merits Peter's initial refusal: "You will never wash my feet" (John 13:8). Jesus here acted intentionally, which he elaborates on a bit later not simply in terms of his actions' immediate significance but also in light of the disciples' mission in the world: "Do you know what I have done to you? You call me Teacher and Lord—and you are right, for that is what I am. So if I, your Lord and Teacher, have washed your feet, you also ought to wash one another's feet" (vv. 12–14).

These varying layers to Jesus's radical act suggest that the work of the disciples consists of working out of the nuances presented above: They are to recognize honestly and realistically that they are not greater than their Teacher and Lord, and they are called to serve one another in a way that dignifies all. With the added notion of washing/purification, this entire event can serve as a metaphor for the way the church is to practice holiness in the world. Holiness involves the church (1) putting into perspective its place before its Lord, (2) recognizing the dignity of others by serving them, and in all of this (3) calling into question those arrangements of privilege, power, and authority that profane the holy name of God and the holiness of God's creatures. The church's holiness, then, pivots on its confession and worship of a holy God as well as its faithful obedience to Jesus's words and faithful imitation of Jesus's actions. Unfortunately, as Jesus readily recognizes, there are those like Judas who hear this call and yet defy it. For these, repentance, confession, forgiveness, and reconciliation are to be sought to the degree possible in this life. But those who actually strive to "work out [their] own salvation with fear and trembling" (Phil. 2:12)—with the full understanding that "it is God who is at work in [them], enabling [them] both to will and to work for God's good pleasure" (v. 13)—are the saints, the church, the holy children of the living God.

THE CHURCH-SCRIPTURE ANALOGY

The church properly confesses itself as a holy people because of its abiding relationship with a holy God. God sanctifies the church's membership as a "holy nation" because it has been chosen and treasured by God, who alone is intrinsically holy (1 Pet. 2:9; see Exod. 19:6; Isa. 43:20–21) and who makes holy and happy a people covenanted with God. While we admit that this ecclesial mark is often obscured by the failures of the church's public witness, we press the point that its confession is not an act of hubris but a worshipful expression of a confident faith in a holy God who has claimed to make this particular people so. The church's holiness is divinely made, not begotten.

God's decision to choose a people and then to abide actively within and for that people is self-willed and a gift of grace. It would be a mistake, however, to understand the church's holiness in passive terms. God has called the church to practice holiness precisely because the God who abides with the church is holy: holiness is the church's faithful response, to partner with God for the demanding and costly work of realizing God's holy purpose in bringing creation back to order. To adapt a Walter Brueggemann phrase, the sanctified church is the strangest thing about the whole world.[12]

The task before us is to offer a typology of Scripture's holiness that presumes to guide its faithful readers in negotiating between the text's compositional (and time-sensitive) origins as a human production and its postbiblical appointment by God's Spirit as Sacred Scripture for its ongoing (and timeless) use in forming faithful followers of "the Holy One of God" (John 6:69). Any strategy of negotiation should steadfastly seek to avoid dualism or reductionism, anything that disconnects God from the sometimes messy process that produced the biblical canon and from modern criticism's honest reading of those authored/edited compositions the church ultimately came to recognize as divinely inspired. After all, sanctification is an operation of divine grace that "thoroughly cleanses ordinary utensils for their honorable use, set apart and prepared for the Master's use for every good work" (2 Tim. 2:21 AT).

The affirmation of Scripture as a holy text is made problematic for reasons roughly analogous to the perceived hypocrisy of the church's self-affirmation as a holy community when reports of sexual abuse

---

12. Brueggemann, *Bible Makes Sense*, 53. His original quote is "The God of the Bible is the strangest thing about the whole Bible."

and bigotry are routinely reported. In the case of Scripture, if the public perceives the holiness of the church's "Holy Bible" as signifying that it is free from error or that its textual meaning is so plainly understood that conflicting applications are avoidable, then they are right to be offended by such an affirmation. Scripture is simply not this.

But our concern is different. The challenge presented by modern biblical criticism is its focus on the communicative intentions of the author, which are subjected to a registry of religious, historical, and literary contingencies of a biblical text believed to be in play at the moment of its origins as an ancient composition. At the very least, Scripture is approached as a common literary production whose referent is its particular socioreligious location in antiquity and whose essential nature is historically understood. If so, then any claim for God's involvement in Scripture's production is dismissed as religiously biased, as is the belief that its Spirit-led interpretation gives expression to God's communicative intentions. The result is what Webster calls "the plunge into dualism,"[13] wherein Scripture is stripped of any divine cast or redemptive purpose, becomes an ancient artifact, and is read as such.

According to Luke's version of the risen Lord's Great Commission, however, his messianic mission as witnessed by his apostles supplies not only the subject matter of the *missio Dei* but also the guarantor of Scripture's discrete witness to this same mission (Luke 24:44–49). The reliability of these two interpenetrating witnesses to the risen Jesus, scriptural and apostolic, is the heartbeat of the church's mission to all the nations. Recall that in the previous chapter we argued that Scripture's unity is made explicit by Jesus's commission to interpret a single canonical book according to the particularity of his life and messianic purpose. The implication of this command is to anticipate a robust intertextuality between the gospels of the prophets (Old Testament) and the gospels of the apostles (New Testament); their diverse parts are ordered by the apostolic witness to Jesus Christ. The crucial idea to take away from this judgment is that the formation of the church's Scripture, New Testament and Old

13. Webster, *Holy Scripture*, 21.

Testament, must not be detached from the messianic hermeneutic that recovers its Christian sense (see Matt. 5:17–20).

The context of Jesus's commissioning of his apostles is important for us to notice. The church's participation in the *missio Dei* to forgive the sins of all the nations is made necessary by the risen Messiah's departure, his mission cut short by Rome's complicity in Israel's rejection of Jesus as God's appointed Messiah. The promise of his return is, in effect, a promise to complete the mission he has begun and so to fulfill all the promises God made to Israel according to Scripture, fulfillment on earth as already in heaven. The role of the church's Scripture and its messianic hermeneutic, then, is limited to this post-ascension moment between the departure of the risen Lord and his return to usher in the promised reign of God on earth as it now is in heaven. Indeed, the prophet Jeremiah reminds us that when this kingdom comes, Scripture will no longer be needed to understand the ways of God because God "will put Torah within them and write it on their hearts and minds. . . . They will no longer need to teach their neighbors or families to know me. For all of them, from the least to the most important, will know me" (Jer. 31:33–34 AT). Simply put, Bible practices are sanctified by God's Spirit with a limited shelf life: these last days of salvation's history bracketed by the two advents of God's Messiah for the work of creation's full restoration.

The consequence of modernity's conception of Scripture's ontology and practice within today's church has been catastrophic, especially for its Protestant communions where the Reformation's *sola Scriptura* is accorded central importance in Christian worship and catechesis. In the traditionally mainline Protestant church, Scripture has long been discredited by a hermeneutics of suspicion, ironically learned by its clergy in preparing for ministry, according to which Scripture typically fails the test of historical reliability and cultural relevance. The shift in the West to a post-Christian zeitgeist is mostly the result of this loss of Scripture's intellectual respectability. Evangelicalism's conservative reaction to this epistemic shift has been to sponsor the opposite reductionism: securing Scripture's ongoing authority and practice by an ontology that views Scripture as propositionally revealed to divinely inspired authors, who were thereby enabled to produce a godlike book.

Our mediating position attempts to keep the human and divine features of Scripture together without resorting to the deeply flawed incarnational typology to do so. On the one hand, we accept the gains of modern biblical criticism as God's gifts in due season to help the church's teachers interpret and apply biblical writings as ordinary human productions subject to our careful linguistic analysis. On the other hand, we also maintain that these same literary productions—however each came to be composed and edited into their canonical form, by and for whomever—were subsequently sanctified by the Holy Spirit and received by the church for their ongoing use as the indispensable auxiliary by which the Spirit forms and reforms God's people into loving communion with a holy God and one another. We distinguish two integral points of Scripture's origin, the first being its composition (a human production), which doubtless was used by the Spirit at the particular locations of its initial reception, and the second being its canonization (a divine reproduction), which sanctified these same texts for continuing use by God's people in every time zone of every age.

Holy Scripture as the Spirit's Auxiliary (John 14–17)

"Sanctification is the act of God the Holy Spirit in hallowing creaturely processes [i.e., Scripture], employing them in the service of the taking form of revelation within the history of the creation."[14] If Scripture's production is understood this way, then its essential nature is not first of all reconstructed with goods retrieved by the competent historian from what remains of a text's origins as a literary "creature," or even from what remains of its postbiblical origins as the church's Scripture. While we affirm the presence and participation of God's Spirit in both these historical movements, we also believe that a theological typology of Scripture's holiness must sound a note, however faint, from a prior moment when the very idea and role of Scripture proceeded from the triune God as a crucial matter of God's providential ordering of God's self-revelation for the work of creation's redemption.[15] In other

---

14. Webster, *Holy Scripture*, 17.
15. Judaism's shibboleth that "in the beginning was Torah" captures this sensibility well.

words, what event occasioned this present, albeit temporary, need for Scripture? What prompted the Spirit to act sometime following Jesus's departure to sanctify a protracted process that produced the final edition of the church's biblical canon centuries later?

By answering these questions, we gain clarity on Scripture as a sanctified text and get a better sense of its divinely intended usefulness in worship, catechesis, and mission. Simply put, the predicate of Scripture's authority is the Spirit's decision regarding which texts, and in what form, would prompt the church's recognition and reception of that text and the church's use of it to gain the wisdom necessary for salvation and the materials that would mature Christian life (see 2 Tim. 3:15–17). Scripture was not begotten by divine dictation but made by the Spirit's sanctification of preexisting textual materials. Again, holiness is who God is; what God does is to sanctify material realities, whether the church or its Scripture, so that as sanctified they may continually serve God's holy ends, no matter the time or place.

In this regard, it is a categorical mistake to suppose that God's holiness separates God's presence from everything else, presumably because God is "wholly other" than everything human. God's sanctifying grace actually targets the distance created between an utterly holy God and all the profanities of human life in order to bridge this gap and enable the church and its Scripture to practice ways of serving God in the world. Scripture's prophetic performances in "showing and correcting mistakes" and its priestly performances in "teaching and training" its faithful readers (2 Tim. 3:16 AT) typify those Bible practices that form a counterculture of holiness. The creaturely fragility of Scripture requires a precision of practice (exegesis, interpretation, application) similar to the protocols prescribed in Leviticus for the priests of Israel in handling sanctified objects, practices that allow texts to perform their formative roles in worship, catechesis, and mission.

Perhaps no passage in the fourfold Gospel tradition is more purposeful in delineating the conditions of discipleship for a post-ascension world than Jesus's farewell discourse, according to John 14–17. The disciples' interrogation of Jesus following the announcement of his imminent departure from them—and, in effect, the abrupt cessation of their discipleship—makes clear to the reader what is at stake. Thomas's poignant question sums up the theological crisis occasioned by Jesus's departure: "Lord, how can we know the way?" (14:5 ΛT). His response is spread out over two sections of the farewell speech, John 14:15–27 and 16:1–15, but aptly summarized in 14:26: "The *Paraclētos*, the Holy Spirit, whom the Father will send in my name, will teach you everything and will remind you of everything I said to you" (AT). Cued by Jesus's departure (16:7), the Spirit will continue Jesus's revelation of God's way, truth, and life (14:6) by teaching his disciples and by reminding them of what the glorified Jesus had said during his earthly ministry (cf. Matt. 28:20).

In light of the risen Jesus's commissioning of his disciples to apply a messianic hermeneutics of Scripture, thereby to fund a biblical witness of God's redemptive plan (Luke 24:44–49), the continuing formation of those who know "everything" about Jesus is a necessary condition of their apostleship. What is at stake in the post-ascension cooperation of the glorified Jesus and the Holy Spirit, whom the Father sends in his place, is the church's future mission as witness to the redemptive work of God through Christ. The Spirit teaches the church what it must know of Jesus in order that it might rightly read Scripture as a reliable witness to God's saving grace.

While there is much debate regarding the relationship between the Spirit's teaching (διδάσκω, *didaskō*) and reminding (ὑπομιμνήσκω, *hypomimnēskō*) ministries,[16] it seems best to understand "teaching" and "reminding" as two discrete but interpenetrating operations of the Spirit to influence and form disciples for a post-ascension setting in which the risen Jesus is humanly absent from them and so is unable to continue his instruction.

What is lacking from this summary verse, however, is any indication of *how* the Spirit will perform these actions, whether directly or indirectly. On the one hand, one finds the stunning claim in 1 John 2:27 that the community's reception of "the anointing" absolves it from further written instruction, since this charismatic experience "teaches you about all things" and therefore seems unmediated and direct (although see 1 John 4:1–6). On the other hand, we are inclined to understand the concluding reference to a written collection of an

---

16. Wiarda, *Spirit and Word*, 121–36.

eyewitness's memories of Jesus (John 21:24–25) as implying its use-fulness as an auxiliary of the Spirit's continuing work to secure the community's belief in Jesus and so realize his promise of eternal "life" with God on this basis (20:30–31; see also 17:2–3). These concluding references to a written deposit recall Jesus's farewell discourse, in which the verb "believe" (14:10–12, 29; 16:9, 27, 30–31; 17:8, 20–21) and the promise of "life" with God (14:6; 17:2–3) are linked to the Spirit's future ministry. This connection strongly suggests that in the post-ascension community following Pentecost, the Spirit has new responsibilities, which are paired with and facilitated by the canonical Gospel.[17]

If the Spirit appointed the Gospel as an auxiliary for disclosing the sanctifying word of truth to teach and guide Jesus's disciples for their mission during this interim period, then we might further ask how this community, which has received this teaching Spirit at Pentecost (John 20:21–23; see also Acts 2:1–4), comes to recognize and canonize the fourfold Gospel the Spirit will use to teach them about Jesus in his absence. Stipulating the criteria of canonization has been a topic of much discussion and debate since the magisterial Reformation. For the purpose of this typology, however, we will continue to follow the lead of the Lord's intercessory prayer in John 17. According to verses 20–23, John's Jesus targets a future when the church's successful mission adds new converts by its ministry of the sanctified word of truth (that is, the canonical Gospel) now in its possession. This Gospel of the Spirit's own choosing may be recognized by its usefulness in producing a certain kind of witness in a post-ascension world that no longer benefits from the historical Jesus's personal presence as God's incarnate Son.

In two particular ways, this passage serves to clarify the church's vocation: (1) Three successive *hina* (ἵνα, "so that," 17:21) clauses

---

17. John's mention of "life" as the ultimate purpose in producing a written memoir of Jesus recalls his farewell prayer, which begins by underwriting this same connection between the reception of "eternal life" and knowing Jesus, through whom "the only true God" is also known (17:2–3). It is this word of "truth" (17:17; cf. 14:6), now remembered by receiving "the Spirit of truth" (14:17; 15:26; 16:13) together with "the words" (17:8) of the gospel story, that teaches disciples about the glorified One who is "the truth" (14:6), which sanctifies Jesus's disciples for their participation in the *missio Dei* (17:17–19).

focus our attention on the compelling witness of a *unified* community whose life together underwrites the risen Son's messianic mission to purify the world of its sin (cf. John 1:29).

(2) The second effect of the community's Spirit-breathed ministry of this sanctified Gospel is its reception of God's "glory" or presence given to them (17:22). The full range of the community's experience of God's indwelling presence may be inferred from the repetition of "glory" in the Gospel. God's glory is disclosed in the works of Jesus (v. 4) as "full of grace and truth" (1:14). The Spirit of truth participates in the glorification of Jesus by continuing to communicate the life of "the Holy One of God" (6:69) to his followers (16:12–16). We take this to be a profoundly trinitarian sensibility in which the glorious presence of the Father, which is self-evidently "full of grace and truth," is instantiated in the works of God's Son, whose apostolic witness is preserved in the canonical Gospel—a sanctified word of truth—for use by the Spirit to sanctify the church for its ministry in the world.

These conclusions shape how we understand canonization as a process of divine providence: the canonical process was a hallowing process by which the church came to recognize those texts appointed and made holy by the Spirit for use in teaching the church that Jesus is the way, truth, and life. The Spirit's current ministry is cued by Jesus's departure and his temporary absence from his followers, who continue to ask Thomas's question: "How can we know the way?" These writings were collected and ordered into a scriptural witness for the church's work in the *missio Dei*. It is by this sacred witness that we know "there is salvation in no one else, for there is no other name under heaven given to people by which we must be saved" (Acts 4:12 AT).

Holy Scripture as "This Jar of Clay" (2 Cor. 3–4)

The second critical element for constructing a typology of Scripture's holiness concerns the proper endgame and so the practices of the church's Scripture, which, as we have claimed, target the formation of a Christlike community within the bounds of its loving communion with a holy God and one another. Scripture's ongoing practice and the history of its effects (*Wirkungsgeschichte*) may also be considered a "hallowing creaturely process."

Paul says this formative process evinces believers who "are being transformed into the same image from one degree of glory to the next, which is from the Lord, who is the Spirit" (2 Cor. 3:18 AT). Although interpreters debate the meaning of his difficult statement, most agree that it concentrates the immediate discussion of apostolic ministry, which he earlier calls a Spirit-funded "ministry of a new covenant" (3:6 AT) and subsequently a "proclamation of the truth" (i.e., "the word of God"; 4:2 AT). He confidently assumes his apostolic ministry (cf. 2:14–3:6), especially when compared to the results of the "old covenant" (3:12–15), since preaching "the glorious gospel of Christ" (4:4 AT) illumines ("lights up") rather than conceals ("veils") the minds and hearts of those who hear it (cf. 3:16–18).

Significantly, Paul grounds this result in his partnership with God's Spirit, whose transformative operations produce "freedom" (3:17) from veiled minds and hardened hearts (3:14–16). The initial effect of the believer's conversion of the imagination is to draw believers ever closer toward God—"from one degree of glory to the next"— whose very material presence (or "glory") can now be experienced by gazing at its reflection in a mirror (3:18). This "mirror" is the striking metaphor, often used by rabbis (see James 1:22–25), for Paul's apostolic ministry and in particular his proclamation of the glorious gospel of Christ. Unlike the photographer or painter whose touch-ups alter the image of what is actually there, Paul's "glorious gospel" is a "mirror" that accurately reflects an unvarnished image of the One who is the real image of God (2 Cor. 4:4). It is a people's reception of this apostolic proclamation of Christ that provides the normative agency for the promised transformation "from one degree of glory to the next"—a hallowing process led by God's Holy Spirit that re-forms believers into the likeness of "the Holy One of God."

To be sure, Paul's apostolic "mirror" proffers only a temporary medium by which believers have access to God's truth—the prolepsis of a future that 1 John describes as a face-to-face encounter of the Son (1 John 3:2; see John 14:9). But in this epistolary setting where the quality of Paul's apostolic goods is being questioned (perhaps by some Jewish opponents in comparison to the synagogue's public reading of Moses; see Acts 15:13–21), Paul's first line of defense is to contend for the effectiveness of his missionary proclamation about Jesus, "the likeness of God," in providing people with a high-quality "mirror" that reflects sound knowledge of God's glory or presence (2 Cor. 4:6). Receiving such theological instruction is the foundation for Christian formation.

The contrast between Paul's confident defense of his apostolic gospel, which he claims is the Spirit-led agency by which people come to know God's glory (4:6), and his modest recognition that this same gospel ministry is contained in a "jar of clay" (v. 7 AT)—this contrast provides an important qualification to the hallowing process discussed above: sanctification is a divinely animated process of ordinary things, of "jars of clay." Biblical images of holiness are often found in passages where sanctified creatures are rubbed raw by their persistent friction with those worldly systems and secular practices opposed to God's will. A recent report from the Barna Group observes that the spiritual disaffection of so many millennials is the result of their perception of Scripture's inability to respond to the issues that concern their intellectual culture (e.g., climate-change science and same-sex marriage).[18] Likewise, we are tempted to add that the biblical hermeneutics of suspicion that guides so much of modern biblical criticism has had a similar effect by weakening the church's grip on Scripture as God's revelatory word. Criticism has surely helped us to better understand the profound creatureliness of biblical texts as authored and edited, as historically and literarily shaped, and as occasionally received and globally institutionalized human productions, but it has done so in a way that often detaches its careful textual analysis from the sanctifying process that transforms these same texts—these "jars of clay"—into auxiliaries of the Spirit for use in forming a faithful people in whom God finds pleasure.

Paul's poignant realization is that his apostolic ministry, while a treasure trove of life-changing goods, is contained in "jars of clay." This image underscores our key point that the Spirit sanctifies ordinary things, such as biblical texts, for an extraordinary service in the divine economy. While Paul's modest admission about his gospel in

18. Kinnaman, *You Lost Me*, esp. 131–47.

2 Corinthians seems a distant cry from his bold declaration in Romans that his gospel is "God's power for salvation to everyone who believes it" (Rom. 1:16 AT), his use of the clay-jar metaphor cuts in two important ways. On the one hand, it denotes a certain fragility: clay easily breaks. On the other hand, clay is easily molded into functional utensils with a wide range of practical uses (see 2 Tim. 2:20–21). This implies something about the human agency of "the word of God" (2 Cor. 4:2 AT): even Paul's proclamation of God's word is like fragile clay, molded, given, and used by frail creatures, any of whom could fail God at any moment (4:16; see also 2 Tim. 2:10–13).

In this case, Paul recognizes that his apostleship deposit is carried around in a fragile jar; it is a fully human venture, subject to the vicissitudes of recurring persecution, physical decline, and temptation, and thus in constant need of spiritual and intellectual renewal (2 Cor. 4:8–11, 16). While the canonical Paul of Acts and the Pauline biography via his canonical letters clearly realize ownership of a consecrated ministry, Paul receives it and gives it away with the full awareness that it requires his own hard choosing at every step of the way: "We believe, therefore we speak . . . and do not give up" (4:13, 16 AT). Readers should not suppose that Paul's ministry of the gospel, and the church that shares in it, is a foregone conclusion: it is a sacred treasure carried in a jar of clay.

This contrast between clay jars and God's glory draws yet another more important contrast between human and divine agency. Its purpose is to show off God's power, not Paul's apostolic authority. In fact, the phrase that concludes this purpose clause in 4:7, καὶ μὴ ἐξ ἡμῶν (kai mē ex hēmōn), recalls that the sanctification of believers into the image of Christ is "from the Lord who is the Spirit" (3:18 AT) and therefore is not the natural effect of merely looking into the "mirror" of the apostolic word. Sanctification is not smoke and mirrors! Yes, God needs apostolic creatures for the Spirit-directed operations of sanctification to succeed. But the source and powerful results of God's sanctifying grace are from and for the glory of God.

We now are prepared to draw this essential element of our analogy: relating Paul's conception of apostolic ministry in 2 Corinthians 3–4 and the reception of Scripture's apostolic writings as the clay jar that God's Spirit has set apart for use in the hallowing process of Christian formation. If we suppose that the canonical referent of Paul's "glorious gospel of Christ" is Scripture's collection of Pauline productions, then we might be able to speak of Scripture as a "mirror" whose reading not only reflects the image of Christ but also, when paired with the Spirit, transforms faithful readers "from one degree of glory to the next."

First of all we should admit that on the rare occasion when biblical writers reflect on their literary art, they do not characterize what they are making as inspired or oracular productions as though they had little to do with them. As authors, they characterize their compositions as conventional, not canonical, literature that is addressed to real people and read aloud to congregations in public worship for their spiritual benefit (see, e.g., psalter superscriptions or epistolary greetings; Luke 1:1–4; Eph. 3:3–4; 1 Tim. 4:13; Rev. 1:3–4). Authors and editors produced literary creatures of their own design and communicative intentions. Only after these texts were written and put into wide circulation and use did the church come to recognize that what was previously preached by apostles and prophets and then published in different forms for changing audiences enjoyed the Spirit's sanctifying presence for all time. These texts were canonized on this basis.

We contend that any close reading of Scripture employs all the tools of biblical criticism to enable faithful readers to a more wakeful understanding of what the text plainly teaches us about God, God's people, and God's world. The aim of exegesis is not to hunt down a privileged meaning of the text according to its author's intention or its first readers' apprehension of it. The penultimate aim is to address a text's lack of clarity as a major cause of its misuse or nonuse among its present interpreters. The goal of exegesis is, within the community of interpreters, to build a consensus of what a text plainly says in anticipation of its possible performances as a transformative text. For this reason, we place a premium on linguistic analysis, in part because we realize that the inherent elasticity of words or the multiple functions of their grammatical relations are responsible for a text's lack of clarity.

As the textual media of the Spirit's progressive sanctification of their faithful readers, it is their very creatureliness that contrasts with the witness of their ongoing effects as the powerful auxiliary of God's Spirit, who uses them to transform faithful readers and hearers into the image of Christ. We have no need to apologize for the occasional artlessness of biblical narrative, nor to harmonize away the textual contradictions and errors of fact sometimes found, nor to set aside the theodicy of some biblical narratives, nor to engage in excessive hand-wringing over any of the other textual and theological problems that tend to offend those who seek after a godlike Scripture. It is the ordinary creatureliness of Scripture that, when contrasted with the powerful, life-transforming effects that issue from its steady use in worship, cate-chesis, and mission, underwrite its enduring authority as a holy book.

CONCLUDING THOUGHTS

That both the church and its Scripture can be spoken of as "holy" is remarkable. Of course, there are challenges with this characteriza-tion, ones that we have tried to account for in our elaboration. But confession of a holy church and a holy word is ultimately a confession of a holy God who puts to use ordinary, creaturely things to achieve God's holy purposes.

Several things are involved with this confession of the Trinity's initiative and work of sanctification. One is that the possibility and potential of creaturely realities are God-given. God calls creaturely beings to be, calls the church to be, and calls biblical texts to be. God is at work at all times and places in making God's world resplendent with the beauty and sanctity of the creator God. As we have stressed throughout, limits are associated with creaturely realities, and these limits can involve a number of matters, including ignorance, errors in human judgment, and so on. When human agency is involved, transgression of those limits into sinfulness is all too common.

And yet, the Trinity has an end for the church and for Scripture: the hallowing of the earth and ultimately the hallowing of God's name. God works in and through the church and Scripture to show the world both its profanity and an alternative: reconciled, holy communion with God. That there are holy people and holy texts is a testament to a holy God's presence, engagement, and work.

5

Catholicity

Confusion abounds when one hears talk of the church's catholicity. Part of the difficulty has to do with specific ecclesial formations. When the descriptor is capitalized, it refers to the Roman Catholic Church. The prominence of the word's tie to this faith communion means that people sometimes equate the two, even if the term is not capitalized. The church we worship at, for example, regularly recites the Apostles' Creed, which includes the confession of belief in the "holy, catholic Church." This local church, like many others, finds it necessary to footnote with the clarifier "universal" so that people are not confused by the term "catholic."

If the church is confessed to be "catholic," and this word is synonymous with the term "universal," what does it mean? On turning to the etymology of "catholic," one notices that its Greek roots suggest "according to the whole." One of the places where this word-phrase is found in Scripture is Acts 9:31: "Meanwhile the church throughout Judea, Galilee, and Samaria had peace and was built up. Living in the fear of the Lord and in the comfort of the Holy Spirit, it increased in numbers." In this translation (NRSV), the word "throughout" is the chosen rendering for the construct *kath holēs* (καθ' ὅλης). One could easily translate the first part of this verse alternatively as, "Meanwhile, according to the whole of Judea, Galilee, and Samaria, the church had peace and was built up." Implied in this phrasing is a sense of fullness and thoroughness, which makes the translation of "throughout" appropriate. The suggestion here is that the church had peace and was built up not simply in one region or location but thoroughly, throughout Judea, Galilee, and Samaria.

The particulars of this passage point to something about catholicity. It is quite fascinating that these three locales are mentioned as having peace and being built up thoroughly, for as any close reader of the New Testament knows, there are some deep-seated regional tensions alluded to in Scripture involving these places. For instance, the story in John 4 of the Samaritan woman whom Jesus encounters at the well points out these differences blatantly; Nathanael's slight of Nazareth in John 1:46 is another example. To make the claim of peace and being built up thoroughly across these locales is significant, given the reality of tensions on the ground.

How can the extension of this analogy to Scripture be made? Are there tensions in Scripture too? What does it mean to take Scripture in a "thorough" or "catholic" way? Many readers of Scripture we encounter have a hard time admitting the inherent complexity within Scripture itself, and "tensions" may be a hard word to introduce to their sense of the Bible's message. Other words are just as or even more difficult, such as "paradoxes" or "contradictions." For some of these believers, Scripture represents truth, and they do not believe there can be any inconsistencies or tensions in truth.

But a hard look at Scripture shows repeated tensions, and these tensions can in turn be mechanisms for securing deep or thought-provoking truths, ones that appear tension-laden on the surface but that may actually lead to more profound insights, maybe even some that go "against the grain," so to speak. This last challenge indicates something important: Scripture's readers may sense tensions, even contradictions, rather than occasions for deep truths on account of their own interpretive imaginations—that is, what they bring to the table of interpretation in terms of what is possible and desirable. The imagination of Scripture's readers should not be downplayed, for it is often powerfully at work, shaped by histories of interpretation and the effects or influences of those texts (*Wirkungsgeschichte*, as noted in the previous chapter), in which certain themes and texts are ignored or relegated to subordinate status whereas others are given special—and sometimes undeserved—privilege. We are all affected by these histories since we are shaped and trained to read Scripture in certain ways by those in our midst (that is, by our contexts). Under such conditions, situations present themselves where what may seem obvious to some readers may be entirely ignored by others. Despite this shaping, which makes it quite natural to highlight some passages and ignore others, it should be recognized that such is not a "catholic" or "thorough" approach.

All in all, there is much to consider when making the ecclesial analogy along the lines of catholicity. There is plenty "throughout" the church and "throughout" Scripture to be accounted for. We aim to point to some of the reasons why a thorough treatment of the church and Scripture does not happen and to some of the possibilities available when we think of God's gracious activity extending throughout all people across the globe and throughout all of Scripture.

PRACTICAL AND DOGMATIC CONSIDERATIONS[1]

Catholicity Is Not Constantinianism

John Wesley, the founder of Methodism, was very quotable in his lifetime. One of his widely known quotes is "The world is my parish." Now, a little background: The remark can be found in a journal entry by Wesley dated Monday, June 11, 1739. Included with the entry is a copy of a letter written to James Hervey, and in this letter we find the quote in question. For the sake of context, this entry is roughly one year after Wesley's famous Aldersgate experience, in which his heart was "strangely warmed" and he was prompted to begin, within a few months, the "scandalous activity" of open-air, field preaching.

The question Wesley was addressing had to do with the propriety of his preaching in the context of parishes other than his own. A rule about this was registered by the Council of Nicaea and repeated

1. Part of this section was presented in modified form as the Weter Lecture at Seattle Pacific University in April 2017. My (Castelo's) thanks to those who support the Weter Lectures for this honor and opportunity.

within the ordinances of the Church of England. Basically, the issue is that this activity was deemed improper, an act of "stepping on other people's [ecclesiastical] tocs."[2] Nevertheless, Wesley felt bound by a "higher authority" to heed the call to preach the gospel and felt justified in doing so on "scriptural grounds." As he reasoned, "God in Scripture commands me, according to my power, to instruct the ignorant, reform the wicked, confirm the virtuous. Man forbids me to do this in another's parish." He continues, "Whom then shall I hear? God or man?" He quotes, among others, Paul from 1 Corinthians— "Woe is me if I preach not the gospel"—and adds in conclusion, "Suffer me now to tell you *my* principles in this matter. *I look upon all the world as my parish*; thus far I mean, that in whatever part of it I am, I judge it meet, right, and my bounden duty, to declare unto all that are willing to hear the glad tidings of salvation. This is the work which I know God has called me to. And sure I am that his blessing attends it."[3] As one can see, the original phrase was a manner of justifying Wesley's ministry since it was unconventional in a certain way. Appeals are made to Scripture—and to divine command, no less—to support the activity. When put this way, how can honoring human custom stand up to heeding God's call?

But let us press to a deeper level. Implicit in this statement is a particular understanding of "world." Also implicit is Wesley's particular self-understanding of his own agency. Put simply, the phrase operates out of the logic that the self is called to make an impact on the world. The world is standing as an open field—in this case figuratively and literally—ready to be influenced by the agency of a single self.

Now let me say from the outset that this Christian understanding of both the self's agency and of the world has generated a number of positive contributions. Throughout Christian history people like Wesley have sacrificed immensely for the cause of Christ by stepping into unknown or unpredictable circumstances to profess "the glad tidings of salvation," which Christians find to be good and worth sharing. Christianity operates out of a mission-oriented ethos, one that is registered in a number of biblical passages, including the Great

---

2. For more on this, see Campbell, "Negotiating Wesleyan Catholicity," 2–4.
3. Wesley, "Journal Entry, 11 June 1739," 67 (emphasis added).

Commission passage of Matthew 28:19–20 ("Go therefore and make disciples of all nations, baptizing them in the name of the Father and of the Son and of the Holy Spirit, and teaching them to obey everything that I have commanded you"). Here in Jesus's words, we are dealing with a command: it is imperative that Christ's followers do this. Likewise, on a personal level I have benefited from this kind of approach. My family on my father's side came to faith in part because of the special call felt and heeded by a woman named Maria Atkinson. The Spirit used Sister Maria powerfully as she suffered for the gospel and took a stand for Christ in her ministry throughout northern Mexico. Therefore I trace part of my Christian lineage back to her, and I am grateful for her obedience to the call of God on her life to "make the world her parish," so to speak.

And yet this understanding of the self and world is not innocuous. In fact, it can be funded by quite a few difficult assumptions, ones that can be self-privileging and other-denying. On the one hand, if a person operates out of the idea that "what I have, other people need," there is potential self-privileging at work. As with all kinds of privilege, a power dynamic can set in, one that can suggest, "I have the resources you need; therefore, you need me and my help." And when coupled with other kinds of privilege, this perspective on how to promote the Christian message can be devastating, with little to no accountability regarding the abuse of power. On the other hand, assumptions can also be at work in this perspective that are other-denying. What we mean by this is that the self can be highlighted to such an extent that alterity (that which is "other") generally is neglected, diminished, silenced, or ignored. This "other" can be other human beings and even God. Again, if the self "has" what others need, then others can easily be phased out of the picture, since the self already is registered with the capacity and means needed to make a difference. If the self is what is ultimately important, then other selves in the world are lessened in terms of their dignity and contributions. These others would include those who are also created in the image of God and could possibly even include God, who dignifies all selves and in whom all things live, move, and have their being.

The reason we highlight this Wesley quote and issues related to self/other dynamics as a way of beginning an ecclesial account of catholicity is that there are plenty of cases throughout history, many admitted by non-Christians and Christians alike, when the people of God have overextended themselves—when they have had an inadequate sense of themselves in terms of their privilege and power as they carried out their call to reach "all" nations. One of the most prominent ways of describing this kind of warped sense of identity and mission has been the label "Constantinianism."

Constantinianism has as its reference Emperor Constantine, or Constantine the Great, who was in power within the Roman Empire during the years 306–37. Much could be said about Constantine. Significant parts of his life and legacy have been debated for years, in part because we have competing accounts from antiquity. People continue to ask: Did he convert to Christianity? If so, where, when, and what kind of conversion was it? The most famous account related to these questions is the vision he and his soldiers allegedly had in 312 just before the Battle of the Milvian Bridge, a vision that included light, a cross, and a voice. But differing testimonies exist even of this particular event.

As one presses into the theological significance of Constantine, one is faced with additional queries. For instance, if he was a Christian, what kind of Christian was he? Here we need to look at what he said and did, and again, the available materials paint a complex picture. He certainly was an ambitious political leader, and throughout his reign he did some terrible things. However, in addition to these acts, he used Christian language quite fluently and knowledgably. When speaking to bishops, for instance, he included first-person-plural language such as "Our Lord," "Our God," and so forth. He started using Christian symbols on coins and on military and regal equipment. He encouraged bishops to move toward Christian unity, and he was able to articulate quite proficiently the outcomes of the Council of Nicaea and how these were opposed to Arianism. In short, what we have here is an exceedingly complex person and legacy.[4]

Before proceeding further, I do want to draw a distinction between the man Constantine and the term "Constantinianism." Given the complexity of Constantine's life and legacy and how these are

---

4. For a detailed study on this score, see Leithart, *Defending Constantine*.

significantly disputed, one could draw a number of mutually exclusive conclusions. And when put into historical perspective, Constantine's life and legacy can be received in a nuanced way. After all, when one compares the conditions for Christians during Constantine's reign with conditions during the reign of his predecessor, Diocletian, it is clear that Constantine represents a dramatic improvement in reducing persecution. Still, the reign of Constantine was not without some challenges, and these have persisted throughout Western civilization in modified forms. Given the rise of such conditions during Constantine's reign, he has become a symbol for them, and so the term "Constantinianism" has risen to circulation.

What is the basic character of Constantinianism? Broadly, the term implies the bringing together of Western political power and Christian religious power in a mutually supporting and beneficial relationship. Interestingly, the roots of (in this case, non-Christian) religious and political alignments precede Constantine in the West and may have been part of the reason Christians were so persecuted by the Roman Empire prior to Constantine: Christians would not offer the sacrifices that were deemed necessary for the Roman Empire's survival and flourishing, given their own commitments to Christ's lordship. With Constantine, the cult of emperor worship and other religious matters were replaced by Christianity, but the underlying assumption continued (and this is crucial): religion and power go hand in hand.

With this alignment of political and religious authority as its source, Constantinianism cultivates a number of detrimental theological consequences, ones that run up against a true sense of catholicity. First, Constantinianism fosters a sense of theological-political exceptionalism, believing that the Christian God has blessed, favored, and supported a particular political arrangement. Therefore, it is assumed, when the empire or nation-state acts, it does so by the will of God and maybe even as God's agent on earth. Those deemed as others in an "us-versus-them" dynamic can thus be characterized as God's enemies, who are evil and require God's judgment, which is to be meted out via the nation-state's actions (usually military in nature). Such scenarios conflate theological providence and political self-justification. The entanglement that ensues from this arrangement can be messy, abusive, and painful.

This kind of exceptionalism leads to a second theological consequence. In Constantinian arrangements, the church loses its ability
to speak and stand against the state when the latter oversteps, over-
reaches, or neglects its role. Symptomatic of this loss is when Christians appeal to the opening verses of Romans 13 to justify particular
political arrangements as God-ordained. Within Constantinianism,
it is difficult to make the case that this passage is not a blanket theological endorsement for all that the nation-state wishes to do. If the
church cannot make an independent case for its witness—if it believes
that the state is justified in all that it does because it is a power ordained by God—then the church loses its essential integrity. Rather
than being a countercultural community that proclaims, in Wesley's
words, the "glad tidings of salvation" provided by a crucified and
resurrected Lord, the church becomes an instrument of the state,
blessing all that the state does.

In reaching back to the theme of this chapter, we can say that
Constantinianism is opposite catholicity. The kingdom of God is
composed of all nations, and in it one nation is not given preeminence
over another. Some might object and say that Israel was favored in
the Old Testament, but this objection fails to account for how Christians are called to think of Israel, especially in light of Christ's coming. As Paul highlights in the Epistle to the Romans, the children of
the promise are God's children, and this promise has been extended
beyond the limits of a "fleshly" Israel. Within salvation history, the
election of Israel served particular ends, and ultimately its purpose
was to be a blessing to the nations. Therefore, Israel as a reworked
Christian theological construct is "for the nations," and its role is
distinct within the parameters of a biblically shaped account of salvation history. As a result, other nation-states cannot claim a similar
mantle, and this mantle does not permit exceptionalism in the Christian account of things.

In contrast to Constantinianism, then, the Christian gospel is
"thoroughly for all"—that is, it is catholic in scope. In being shaped
by this gospel, the kingdom of God allows for possibilities not available within Constantinian arrangements. In the latter, survival, power,
and preeminence are all favored, but in the kingdom of Christ, cru-
ciformity, peace, and long-suffering are desirable and in some sense

necessary. Whereas Constantinianism highlights others as potential enemies of the state, the kingdom of God highlights others as God's creatures. The difference between enemy destruction and enemy love could not be starker. Constantinianism and catholicity stand as antithetical alternatives for the church's presence in the public realm.

The Work of the Trinity across the Globe

If catholicity is not Constantinianism, then what is it? Sometimes the appeal to catholicity has been made so as to secure a sense of commonality of belief in light of evident threats to a shared sense of Christian identity. Once again, this approach can easily derail and become an "us-versus-them" dynamic that gives preeminence to "us" and mischaracterizes "them" for the sake of expediency. With this danger acknowledged, however, there is something to be said for a sense of identity and cohesion that helps lift up people beyond their native contexts and surroundings, freeing them to recognize the face of God in the stranger. And that possibility, we reckon, is available in the manifest and powerful work of the Trinity across the globe.

It should not be a secret anymore that Christianity is currently going through a massive growth spurt across the so-called global South while at the same time experiencing serious decline in the transatlantic North. That these developments are happening concurrently in our lifetime is quite remarkable. For those of us in the transatlantic North, it may be hard to understand what is going on in other parts of the world when, in our own contexts, it is quite obvious why Christianity is faltering. One aspect of this decline is that secularism is progressively creating conditions that make faith in a Christian God (or any other outright god, for that matter) less and less possible or appealing. This pressure is not spawned simply by busyness or technology; rather, it rests on complex accounts of how we have been shaped to think of our world, ourselves, and our place within it.

As a reflection of this conditioning, we in the North may find it difficult to understand what is occurring in the South. But let us be clear: what is happening in our day is simply unprecedented. According to a 2011 study by the Pew Research Center, two-thirds of the global Christian population lived in Europe in 1910, but by 2010, this percentage had dwindled to just over one-fourth. During this same period, Christians in sub-Saharan Africa went from making up just 9 percent of the population to making up 63 percent. Overall, in terms of North and South globally, there are 860 million Christians compared to 1.3 billion, respectively.[5]

When looking at these massive and rapid changes, Northerners may appeal to patronizing arguments. One such argument is that the South "has not yet grown up," that they have not experienced a necessary feature of development that the North has experienced—that is, a kind of enlightenment away from "mythological" ways of thinking. Another argument, tied to the first, blames the South for being syncretistic and claims that the Christianity growing in the South is often less "refined" than the versions of Christianity in the North. The argument could be something like this: "Of course Christianity is growing there; it is just meshing with whatever is already in the culture." With such narrations one senses a note of self-granted preeminence on the part of the North, a thorough inability to recognize the legitimacy of alternatives, in this case the possibility of other ways of being Christian besides a known one.

But more is at stake than just a kind of hospitality toward other cultures and other ways of practicing Christianity. At stake is also the ability to recognize the work of God—that is, what the Trinity is doing in the world today. Looming in the background of this phenomenal growth in the global South is a lingering question: Is this the work of the Christian God, the God whom Christians in the global North worship Sunday after Sunday? In other words, is the God of Christian confession and worship behind the growth we are witnessing among Christians of the global South? And if so, what does that mean for those of us in the transatlantic North?

These are difficult questions, to be sure. They are difficult in part because they raise the prospect of leveling the preeminence and privilege that Christianity has enjoyed in Western civilization since the days of Constantine. If the Christian God is working powerfully throughout the globe in unprecedented ways, and the transatlantic

5. Pew Research Center, "Global Christianity."

North (which most likely constitutes the majority of this book's readership) somehow has difficulty accounting for this work, what does this say about the state of Christianity in the North? Would this situation imply that Christianity is at odds with itself in certain contexts? Could it mean that the transatlantic North may need to learn from the global South how to see the Trinity at work in the twenty-first century?

The proof, so to speak, is in the fruits. All Christians of all persuasions must reckon with the claim that the gospel is good news, that it really makes a difference in people's lives. When things are happening in distant places and lands today that are similar to what was reported in the early church, we should recognize a corollary and connection. The power of the cross and resurrection is still evident today. Christian martyrs are still to be found. People continue to heed the call of Christ to become his disciples, and people still actively walk according to the Spirit and not the flesh.

In short, catholicity is a function of the presence and work of the Trinity across the globe. Catholicity is not a clever manipulation of political power, nor does it mean a kind of privilege or preeminence secured by those who are in control. Rather, it is a mark of the community that lives in the active power of the resurrected Lord—the community that illustrates bodily what is referred to in Scripture textually.

Being Catholic Christians

It is an occasion for joy to recognize that the presence and work of God are on display throughout the globe. But at the same time, it is difficult to hear phrases such as "the epicenter of the future of Christianity is shifting" when we know that the places it is shifting to are remote and distant. Of course, God is not limited by space or distance. The God at work in those places is the same God confessed and worshiped during Sunday morning services in the transatlantic North. When one looks beyond the sweeping narratives, one can tell that there are centers and movements of renewal in the West that do not receive major headlines. Yet I repeatedly encounter students who go on various mission trips only to come back with very mixed feelings. They know that something is different about the experience of

God in the places they visit as contrasted to their own hometowns and contexts, but they have a hard time pinpointing what that difference is. They raise questions such as these: Are people more receptive to the gospel in certain contexts? Is God judging the West somehow? Why is it so hard to be a Christian here in the West? And so on.

Again, no easy answers present themselves to such questions, but in the United States in particular recent events have raised the importance of catholicity in the public square, and these may hint at some workable hypotheses for the state of things my students are critiquing. The 2016 election of Donald Trump to the presidency was premised in part on a message of "America first" and "making America great again" (which raises all kinds of questions as to what kinds of "losses from greatness" are being considered and who is said to be affected and responsible). The statistics associated with white evangelical Christians who supported Trump's candidacy are staggering.[6] Obviously, white evangelicals saw in Trump a candidate who would represent some of their prized views and secure for them some kind of political power and influence. The melding of political power and religious persuasion of this magnitude is just one further example of a kind of Constantinian situation, an alliance in which faith and politics can benefit from one another.

One of the difficulties coming out of the election is the way "others" besides white evangelical Christians have felt in light of what the administration has actively said and done (and what has been left undone and unsaid). In these polarized times, quite a few people, including quite a few Christians, feel left out of the political orbit and, in certain cases, even discriminated against or neglected. These are difficult times, yet they offer the Christian church an opportunity to make clear its witness and to come clean about where its allegiances lie. Put another way, the Christian church in the United States is being actively challenged with just how "catholic" it presently is and wishes to be. And the consequences coming from this challenge will necessarily affect both the integrity and the vitality of its witness.

6. Sarah Pulliam Bailey, "White Evangelicals Voted Overwhelmingly for Donald Trump, Exit Polls Show," *Washington Post*, November 9, 2016, https://www.washingtonpost.com/news/acts-of-faith/wp/2016/11/09/exit-polls-show-white-evangelicals-voted-overwhelmingly-for-donald-trump.

To put the matter bluntly, a church committed to catholicity is bound to be marked by renunciation and receptivity. In contexts where the church is populous and influential, the Constantinian temptation will always present itself. It need not be heeded in order to be culturally or politically relevant, even though arguments to the contrary abound. But let it be clear: when that temptation is faced, plenty is at stake in terms of how the church subsists and defines itself. If the church is committed to its Lord, then no alternative savior is needed. If the church is to embody the kingdom of God on earth, then its alliances cannot be exclusively with one nation-state, order, or political party. The work of God and God's purposes simply cannot be limited in such ways. When they are, something is out of order, something of the gospel has been lost.

As drastic as the statistics are, in terms of both the decline of Christianity in the transatlantic North and its rise in the global South, it may still be the case that such conditions prove to be an insufficient wake-up call for the church in the West to receive the gifts of God's work beyond its borders. This would constitute an ultimate kind of judgment. But a recommitment to the church's catholicity can suggest the following: as Christians, we can all learn from one another what it means to worship the Christian God; in fact, we need one another in order that our witness may be true and faithful to our Lord.

The Church-Scripture Analogy

The church's catholicity has mostly been understood in geographical terms: it is the "church universal" whose borders extend to every nook and cranny of planet Earth. No single individual is excluded from its membership based on a street address. In fact, unlike Old Testament Israel, whose distinctive national identity is defined in part by the borders delineated by God's promise of land to Abraham, the church's geographically shaped identity is missional (e.g., Acts 1:8), and its principal boundary markers are confessional (e.g., Rom. 10:9). After all, Paul locates every Christian "in Christ," where their professions of faith and faithful practices distinguish them from those outside of Christ, wherever and whenever a congregation of believers is found (see Rom. 12:9–21).

The inclusivity of the membership of a global church is sometimes given a theological upgrade by the claim that its missional vocation is coextensive with God's creation. The *missio Dei*, then, has a cosmic reach, even extending to the invisible "powers and principalities" of "cosmic darkness" (Eph. 6:12 AT), to whom the church announces the victory of God (3:10; see 1 Pet. 3:19). In this sense, the ecclesial mark of oneness includes this same spatial sense: the church's unity extends to all of creation and can't be restricted to a particular region or ethnic group. There is but one holy church throughout the cosmos. For this reason, God's promise of land and family to Abraham and Sarah, which is the central trope of divine blessing in the Old Testament, is spiritualized and universalized in the New Testament (see Rom. 9:6–13).

As we mentioned at the beginning of this chapter, this expansive conception of catholicity is already cued by Luke's use of καθ᾿ ὅλης (*kath holēs*), which targets an entire geographical region typically translated "throughout" (Acts 9:31; see also Luke 4:14; 23:5; Acts 9:42; 10:37). On close reading, however, Luke's narrative world is constructed of a much thicker conception of a geographical region. To illustrate, when those living in Seattle refer to the "Pacific Northwest," they have in mind a way of thinking, a dress code, an exuberance for recreating and creating—a peculiar manner of life that is distinctively "Northwest." When Luke notes particular places, the story itself carefully circumscribes them as physical locations where certain divine actions are witnessed, where ecclesial practices are performed in response to God's benefaction, and where a providential agency is at work in space and time to accomplish God's holy ends.

The syntax of Acts 9:31 implies that the "peace" that extends "throughout" the church of Roman Palestine, which is built up through Peter's mission to the household of Israel beyond Jerusalem (see vv. 31–43), is the likely effect of Paul's recent evacuation for Tarsus (see vv. 29–30).[7] In this case, the church's experience of calm in this

---

7. The verse's syntax suggests that Acts 9:31 should be read in two parts. The first part, Ἡ μὲν οὖν ἐκκλησία καθ᾿ ὅλης τῆς Ἰουδαίας καὶ Γαλιλαίας καὶ Σαμαρείας εἶχεν εἰρήνην οἰκοδομουμένη (*Hē men oun ekklēsia kath holēs tēs Ioudaias kai Galilaias kai Samareias eichen eirēnēn oikodomoumenē*), is clearly linked by the connecting phrase Ἡ μὲν οὖν ἐκκλησία (*Hē men oun ekklēsia*), to the preceding text and to Paul's departure from the region. Therefore, the peace enjoyed by the church throughout the region is the result of Paul's departure from it (and presumably the

region results from the absence of Paul, whose Spirit-filled proclamation that Jesus is God's Son provoked unrest (v. 26). Without making too much of this irony, we suspect the tension between the missions of Paul and Peter to which Acts 9:31 alludes, which is resolved only by the Spirit's dramatic intervention and Peter's conversion according to Acts 10, marks out the church's catholicity by what is present and also by what is absent in the particular places of its residency.

We contend that this conception of the church's catholicity is analogous to Scripture's catholicity in two ways. First, Scripture's sanctified authority, its inspired usefulness and formative effects, extend to the baptized membership of every congregation of Christ's global church without exception. Second, every Scripture without exception is appointed by God's Spirit as a textual witness to the risen Messiah and is therefore useful in forming a knowing and loving relationship with him. Scripture is a precisely circumscribed witness, a whole gospel for the whole church. To marginalize one member of either body, ecclesial or textual, is to undermine God's intentions for Scripture's variegated practice in a congregation's worship, catechesis, mission, and personal devotions. Implicit in this conception of catholicity is the Spirit's role in resolving tensions between biblical witnesses, thereby enabling one communion of saints to hear a word from God that it hitherto had silenced or was unprepared to receive.

A Catholicity of Readers

Every faith community, whether East or West, North or South, receives the church's Scripture as a special *via media*, or middle way, a trustworthy witness of God's word for God's people. Even a cursory

---

silencing of his provocations described in vv. 26–29). The second half of the verse introduces Peter back into the narrative, and his story in Acts continues in vv. 32–43. The following account of Peter's conversion to God's plan of universal salvation that includes repentant (even though unclean) Gentiles, such as Cornelius (Acts 10), may indicate that the Peter-led church of this region (see 9:31b) is simply unprepared for the catholicity of Paul's witness to Christ in the mode of 9:15–16. When read within this wider narrative context, then, the mention of "peace" in v. 31 is ironic since it envisions a yet unresolved tension between the respective missions of Paul and Peter. It is not until the Gentile Pentecost of Acts 10 that Peter finally understands God's redemptive plans, already disclosed to Paul in 9:15–16.

history of Scripture's reception, while certainly uneven, demonstrates the global scope of its authority and practice. Further, Scripture's translation into the exotic languages of obscure tribes with the intent to mediate God's word even to those groups found on the margins of the two-thirds world confirms Scripture's global reach. The routine reports received by different congregations from their missionaries testify to the effects of translated texts to communicate the power of God for salvation to unknown others.

To elaborate this observation, we note that the first historian of the canonical process, Eusebius, writes of the existence of a second collection of letters, which he titles "catholic."[8] Its textual members are non-Pauline writings in their provenance and are linked to the apostolates of the Jerusalem "pillars" (see Gal. 2:9), thus also to the early church's mission to Israel according to Acts 1–15.[9] Perhaps also cued by Irenaeus's reading of Acts as Scripture, which underscored the importance of Paul's mission to the nations and so implicated the Pauline canon as indispensable for the church's Christian formation, Eusebius went on to observe that the church's reception of this letter collection within the early church was "disputed," certainly in comparison with the Pauline canon.[10] While such a comparison suggested a difference between the two collections' respective authority, Eusebius secured this difference—not without irony—to the restricted geographical circulation and so inspired uses of the so-called catholic

8. The final moment in this plotline is provided by Eusebius (ca. 263–339), who is the first to observe the existence of a Catholic Epistles collection in the East (*Ecclesiastical History* 2.23.25). He was more cautious about the authority of James, 2 Peter, 2–3 John, and Jude, not because of their apostolic content but because they lacked "catholicity" of circulation. Nonetheless, he is the first to call the collection of seven the "Catholic Epistles," which cued its inclusion in the canon lists of the Greek East beginning in the fourth century.

9. There is manuscript evidence that Acts was placed with the Catholic Epistles collection to form a discrete volume of Scripture, called the *Apostolos*, early in the canonical process. Even though the final redaction of the New Testament canon divided one from the other to create a different shape for a different end, this earlier edition of the Catholic Epistles collection is suggestive of the ongoing interpretive relationship between the canonical biographies of James, Cephas (i.e., Peter), and John (Gal. 2:9) in Acts and their canonical letters.

10. The final placement of Hebrews between the two letter collections as a member of neither suggests a role within the New Testament that purposefully moderates the ongoing intracanonical conversation between the two.

collection of apostolic letters within the whole church. The doubt he expressed was over not their orthodox content but the scope of their effective practice.

The irony of Eusebius's use of "catholic" for this disputed collection of epistles is underscored by the Nicene Creed's assigning of this term as one of four identifying marks of the "one holy catholic and apostolic church." We take it that what Eusebius had in mind for a "catholic" collection of writings is roughly the same as what the Nicaean episcopacy had in mind when marking out the public boundaries of the one, holy, apostolic church as catholic: that is, in both cases the catholicity of the church and its biblical canon turns on their geographical reach and the reasonable presumption of their effectiveness in forming a diverse people belonging to God, irrespective of the particularities of their social locations.

The logical connection Eusebius made with the limited geography of a writing's circulation, which thereby limited the scope of its performances within a truly catholic church's worship and catechesis, underwrites our working assumption that a scripture's ecclesial address and practice must necessarily extend to the diverse membership of every Christian congregation. In fact, the effect of Scripture's canonization was to universalize the particular circumstances of each letter's first address as applicable to the locations of every congregation in any age.[11]

The importance of this element of Scripture's catholicity is typically registered, even if sometimes with overdetermined import, by modern criticism's attentiveness to the "original" meaning of biblical texts.[12] Criticism's application of historical and linguistic tools

11. Even though the church brought these writings together to form a discrete canonical collection, they are called "catholic" for metatheological reasons. But the ancient rubric used for this collection has been recently problematized on literary grounds. If "catholic" refers to the geographical scope of the letters' original address, or perhaps to the encyclical intent of their literary genre, then we also have problems with the use of "catholic" to name this canonical collection. The intended audiences of 1 Peter and certainly 2–3 John seem to be more congregational than "catholic" in scope; and the literary genre of 1 John (and some would add James) is not that of an encyclical "epistle" but more like a sermon or treatise intended for insiders of the community of the "beloved disciple" (for more on the beloved disciple, see chap. 6 below).

12. See Barton, *Nature of Biblical Criticism*.

to determine the most likely meaning intended by a text's author/ editor for his first audience is based on the prior reconstruction of that audience's particular social location and the crisis that occasioned the book's composition in the first place. But the postbiblical canonization of Scripture as a collection of interpenetrating canonical collections no longer targets first audiences reading texts according to the intentions of their (typically unknown) authors. Scripture is now read according to the church's intentions, and so its faithful interpretation targets present readers located in an ever-changing social world, where new challenges require a fresh word from God. Sharply put, the catholicity of Scripture requires interpretive practices that problematize historical criticism's presumption that a text's original meaning (that is, the meaning intended by its author for its first audience) is also a text's normative meaning. The orientation an interpreter brings to a faithful reading of Scripture presumes that its sanctified texts are able to transcend the very contingencies of time and space that produced them and thus communicate a relevant reading for a particular community of God's people.[13]

One of the most evocative biblical images of the all-inclusive boundaries of catholicity is the vision of the great crowd in Revelation 7. Gathered here at history's conclusion is an international,

---

13. Robert Gundry has recently argued that the Peter of Matthew's Gospel is portrayed as an apostate whom Jesus denies, not as the apostle whom Jesus rehabilitates and who is featured elsewhere in the fourfold Gospel and Acts; in fact, he is appointed by Luke's Jesus as the lead pastor of the apostles, whom the Lord enthrones to judge Israel (Luke 22:28–34); see *Peter: False Disciple and Apostate*. Gundry's recognition of the problem his study provokes, especially for his own conservative evangelical Protestant communion, is based on his historical-critical presumption that the author's intentions are theologically normative for his future readers—indeed, Gundry believes these authorial intentions are divinely inspired. If, however, we shift the Spirit's activity of sanctifying biblical texts (e.g., Matthew's Gospel) for their enduring use as the church's Scripture from the point of their composition to the postbiblical point of their canonization (i.e., shift from Gundry's approach to Webster's), then Gundry's thesis strikes us as impossible to sustain. In his concluding, awkward attempt to redeem the practical value of his study, Gundry misses the salient point altogether: The church would never have recognized a canonical Matthew, nor would the Spirit have appointed it as such, if it were to contain the biography of a heretical Peter (within an otherwise coherent fourfold Gospel) yet then be read alongside his canonical letters that follow!

diverse community that together celebrates the victory of God. They all are gathered before the Lamb in common garb—white gowns washed clean by the Lamb's blood—and use the same liturgical gestures to worship and bless God. Despite their social diversity, their roots underscore a common history: They have all come from "great hardship" (7:14 AT) and stand in the shelter of the throne to find unending food and drink and relief from the scorching sun (vv. 15–16). The Lamb who has purified them now stands in their midst to comfort and lead them. This lovely picture reminds us that the church's catholicity is grounded in this common hope of a people made whole by the mercies of God.

Another implication of this pivot point extends the metrics used to measure the quality of a translation of Scripture to include, besides its accuracy for catechetical purposes and aesthetics for public reading in worship, whether it makes Scripture more accessible to an inclusive audience of readers and hearers. A church catholic includes members from diverse locations, socioeconomic groups, political affiliations, ages, and religious experiences. A good translation communicates God's word to all God's people.

More importantly, Scripture's practice must retrieve meaning that is universally applicable to a Christ-centered life with God. Perhaps the definitive passage in support of this contour of Scripture's catholicity is Luke's version of the risen Jesus's Great Commission (Luke 24:44–49). Similar to the other Gospels, Luke's concludes with a series of personal encounters between the risen Jesus and his stunned disciples (see Matt. 28:16–20; Mark 16:14–20; John 20:19–23).[14] These encounters climax in a teachable moment that includes the Lord's command for his disciples to engage in a global mission to continue what he has begun and said.

What is especially remarkable about Luke's distinctive witness to this event is the role he grants Scripture. In Jesus's presence as resurrected Lord and by his instruction, what is written in Scripture opens the eyes of the disciples to his true identity as Messiah and to the real results of his mission to save creation from death's sting. According

14. For a brilliant exposition of this idea, see Barth, *Church Dogmatics*, III/2, 468–74.

to Luke 24:27, Jesus retells the story of his passion, pointing out that "all that Moses and the prophets have written are about me" (AT). Luke reports that as he taught Scripture over a shared meal of broken bread, "the disciples' eyes were *opened* and they recognized him" (v. 31 AT).

This eye-opening experience is described by the verb διανοίγω (*dianoigō*), which is repeated in the very next verse when the disciples testify to each other, "Did not our hearts burn within us when [Jesus] opened [διανοίγω, *dianoigō*] scripture to us?" (v. 32 AT). The intellectual capacity of the Lord's first students to understand his resurrection and prior political execution, perhaps even a dawning awareness of its radical implication for their discipleship, is shaped by Jesus's self-referential method of reading Israel's scripture. Not only Scripture itself but also a particular way of reading Scripture is what blows their minds.

The final stop of this Emmaus road trip, of course, is heaven; but right before his exaltation Jesus exploits one final teachable moment. In Luke's distinctive witness to it, the Great Commission does not frame Jesus's departure as a cessation of discipleship but rather the beginning of a new phase, which Acts refers to as the "last days" of salvation's history. It is a liminal moment for the disciples, whose way forward without Jesus was not yet made clear. The Great Commission speaks God's compass into their unsettling moment.

For our purposes, one key element from this passage supports our understanding of Scripture's catholicity.[15] Jesus reminds his disciples that a pedagogy of Scripture is detached neither from him nor from the mission he commands. Disciples are called to proclaim a Scripture-shaped gospel about Jesus to all the nations. This global mission is not just one among several themes that order Scripture's metanarrative; Jesus makes it thematically central to and historically generative of it all. Scripture is performed, practiced, and paraded in service of God's global mission, in which the church participates to save creation from death.

15. Several excellent commentaries on Luke's Gospel provide informed expositions of this passage, especially in relationship to the other versions of this episode in the fourfold Gospel tradition. For theology, see Green, *Gospel of Luke*; for history, see Bovon's three-volume *Luke*.

A Catholicity of Texts

Besides emphasizing Scripture's intention of leaving no faithful reader behind in their Christian formation, catholicity also envisages the simultaneity of Scripture. Featured in Jesus's Great Commission in Luke's Gospel is his christological hermeneutics of Scripture (Luke 24:44), which then shapes the gospel his apostles are to proclaim among the nations. Here the peculiar formulation of Scripture— Torah, Prophets, and Psalms—anticipates the subsequent division of Israel's Tanakh into three volumes, thus departing from Scripture's more typical division into two parts, Torah (that is, "Moses" or "Law") and Prophets (see Luke 24:27; Acts 26:22). At the very least, the storyteller's change of terminology intensifies the all-inclusive scope of Scripture's witness to the risen Jesus's messianic mission— a catholicity of sacred texts, each of which has the Spirit-enabled potential to teach the world about Jesus.

Surely Paul has something like this in mind by asserting that "every scripture" is useful for the practices of Christian formation (2 Tim. 3:16 AT). In this seminal passage about Scripture's inspiration, the singular phrase *pasa graphē* (πᾶσα γραφή, "every scripture") shifts from the preceding plural *hiera grammata* (ἱερὰ γράμματα, "holy writings," v. 15). Paul gives no reason for this change, and the meaning of the terms he uses is ambiguous and remains contested. Although the history of these two terms in Judaism indicates that they are not interchangeable, we do not find a compelling reason to think Paul has a different text in mind by *graphē* than by *hiera grammata*: both terms refer to Israel's scripture in Greek translation. What remains syntactically significant is the change of number from pluriform texts (*grammata*) to a singular one (*graphē*). Whenever an adjective (i.e., *pasa*) is placed with a singular anarthrous noun (i.e., *graphē*), it generally refers to a specific thing ("every") rather than to a collective whole ("all"). If this Pauline affirmation glosses the commissioning statement of Luke's Jesus, then we may construct a typology that envisages every text from every part of Scripture as useful for cultivating a wisdom that saves the nations (see v. 15).

This reading coheres to rabbinical thinking that every part of Scripture holds a word from God. In fact, Rabbi Akiva regulated his readings of Scripture by the *ribbui-mi'ut* ("inclusion-exclusion") rule, which stipulated that even the most familiar and therefore seemingly least significant grammatical particles (e.g., "and," "or," "the," "a") could hold important meanings since by these particles God discloses those included or excluded from covenant blessings. Paul's phrase "every scripture" implies its substantive simultaneity, so that even though its writings are formed in different genres or shaped by different theological ideas, "every scripture" bears common witness to the truth about God, the only God.

Likewise, early disciples such as Ignatius and Clement make a Pauline conception of Scripture clearer by contending that when the church formed its biblical canon, the word "catholic" likely would have denoted a *whole* or *complete* apostolic witness of the historical Jesus, in large part to distinguish it from its nonapostolic rivals.[16] In fact, the consistent orthodoxy of confessing congregations was used interchangeably with catholicity in antiquity; that is, a common theological grammar and set of moral practices among congregations evinced their membership in the church catholic.

In a similar way, the coming together of the biblical canon's final form indicated its completeness as a self-sufficient witness to God's word. From this perspective, the addition of a "catholic" collection of apostolic letters to a still inchoate New Testament canon completed it, both aesthetically and theologically. In particular, given the pervasive concern about protecting an apostolic (that is, "catholic") reading of the fourfold Gospel witness to Jesus and the Pauline canon against their many heretical readers, the church would have received this second collection of letters (perhaps along with Acts) as a canonical safeguard against any theological or moral misuse of the fourfold Gospel tradition and, especially, the canonical collection of Pauline Letters. We should recall that 2 Peter tells us so in 3:15–16! To catholicize the biblical canon, the church needed to add bits to it that would complete it in a way that guarantees the orthodoxy of its use as well as the universal scope of its application.

We observe that the triumph of Pauline Christianity, especially observed within the various Protestant communions of the magisterial

---

16. Ignatius, *To the Smyrnaeans* 6.2; Clement, *Stromata* 7.17.107.

Reformation, has had the effect of either flattening the subject matter of some non-Pauline letters to facilitate their uneasy compliance with a Pauline theological grammar (e.g., Hebrews, 1 Peter) or marginalizing others from serious attention for a fully New Testament theology (e.g., James, 2 Peter). Our anecdotal evidence suggests that this studied disregard of these "neglected" texts in the theological education of clergy has shaped a bias against their use in parish worship, catechesis, and mission.[17] Even when the lectionary, for example, includes New Testament lessons from non-Pauline and deutero-Pauline books, they are rarely the focus of the church's preaching or teaching ministry and are typically ignored—at least in my experience—even when appointed for ecclesial use to thicken the canonical context for hearing God's word in the gospel of Christ. One may assume that this disregard is typically justified for critical reasons.[18]

Among the well-known casualties of this reductionism in Protestantism is the canonical Letter of James, especially its signal passage on the relationship between a believer's profession of orthodox faith (2:14–20) and works of righteousness (2:21–26). When introduced and framed by the traditional "Jewish" concerns registered by the James of Acts regarding the initiation of repentant Gentiles into a covenant-keeping community (Acts 15:12–21, 22–29), not only is the letter's distinctive witness to God's way of salvation made more clear (and by implication, that of the entire catholic collection it

17. In the epilogue to a recent collection on the New Testament's "neglected letters," I argue that this imbalance is instantiated from the very beginning of the canonical process. It is a *canonized* imbalance and so is normative of their reading and use. This imbalance becomes problematic when canonical letters such as 2 Peter, 2 Timothy, or 2 John are neglected altogether in a congregation's Bible practices for worship and instruction. See Robert W. Wall, epilogue to Hockey, Pierce, and Watson, *Muted Voices*, 199–210.

18. Anthony Robinson and I were told by publishers that our proposed book on the Pastoral Epistles, despite the relevance of its core theme (congregational leadership) for today's readers, would have difficulty attracting readers (especially among Robinson's mainline ministerial colleagues in America) whose seminary education has turned them against these biblical books. On the other hand, as a criterion for the book's usefulness, more conservative readers tend to look for agreement on a variety of historical-critical issues (e.g., Pauline authorship), which are mostly indeterminate and add little to a careful exegesis of the biblical text.

introduces), but in this regard so also is its relationship to the preceding Pauline witness.

The James of Acts exemplifies the importance of practicing Scripture to resolve intramural squabbles within a congregation that aspires to a unity of "heart and soul" (cf. Acts 2:42–47; 4:32; 6:1–7). Perhaps the narrator is responding to a nascent Marcionism within his own church, fostered in large part by the failure of the church's mission to Israel and the success of its mission among Gentiles, which is only deepened by the anti-Semitism resident in the Roman world of antiquity. Against the "gentilizing" tendency that marginalizes the church's Jewish legacy (i.e., reading Scripture on Sabbath; 15:21) and accommodates other religious practices that may subvert the church's public identity within a pervasively pagan world (15:20), the James of Acts interprets the relevant meaning of the prophetic texts for his congregation in practical terms (see Acts 15:15–19) and then writes that his findings "seemed good to the Holy Spirit" (v. 28). This confirmation of the Spirit's witness to God's word implies that when James is read together with Acts as Scripture's witness to God's word, these same concerns of the James of Acts frame and freight the contribution James makes within the New Testament canon.

The narrative of James in Acts 15 supplies an important context for reading the Letter of James as Scripture. Significantly, the density of purity language in James (e.g., 1:21, 27; 2:9–11), especially when coupled with quotations and loud echoes from Leviticus and other Jewish writings that touch on a covenant-keeping community's halakhic requirements,[19] resonates with the concern for social purity expressed by the James of Acts (e.g., 15:20, 29; 21:25). In fact, the regulatory norms of corporate life given in the Letter of James are cast in "insider-outsider" terms (e.g., 1:27; 2:2–7) in a way that continues the subtext of James's halakhic midrash in Acts 15:20, supported by clear allusion to the Levitical injunctions regulating Israel's social relations with its unclean neighbors (Lev. 17–18).[20] What seems also clear is that religious practice, choosing to abstain from pagan conventions (Acts 15:20) and embrace a Jewish pattern of worship (v. 21),

---

19. See Johnson, *Letter of James*, 34–46.
20. Bauckham, "James and the Gentiles."

is not viewed by James as a condition of salvation but rather as its social, public expression (v. 19). Consistent, then, with the pattern of conversion found in Acts, being cleansed from sin (2:38; 3:19) in prospect of eternal life (13:46) is the experience of those who repent, whether Jew or Gentile; the community's religious practices (2:42) mark out its common life as "graced" by God's presence (2:47; 4:33) mediated through God's Spirit (2:38). A repentant response to the "word of God" about Jesus and purity/social practices are not causally related but represent deliberate and distinct properties of the community's religious life together.

Likewise, according to the epistolary James, the community's faithful reception of the "word of truth" and "putting away of all filth" (James 1:21 AT) are discrete, deliberate choices of the repentant "soul" that form a whole witness to the righteousness of God. In this symbolic world, "religion that is pure and undefiled," uncontaminated by the anti-God world order, is characterized by religious acts (1:27, θρησκεία/thrēskeia = thrēskeuein)—caring for the poor and powerless in obedience to God's law (Acts 2:43–44; 4:32–35; 6:1–8)—while mere professions of faith are judged "vain" (James 1:26 AT; see also 2:14–20). There is no bifurcation of "heart" religion from the performance of public service, nor is one the logical cause of the other; each is the mutual complement or concrete evidence of the other (2:22, 26). While James has unmistakable eschatological commitments and concerns, so that divine judgment—whether the community has the faith of Jesus (2:1)—is rendered upon evidence (or lack) of obedience to God's law (vv. 8–13), his pastoral intent is equally unmistakable: there are impoverished believers who presently lack justice (vv. 2–7) and material goods (v. 15; see 1:27), and whose very existence depends on the rest of the community's obedience to God. The social and spiritual well-being of the eschatological community depends on the performance of those public practices that mark out its faith as the "faith of the Lord Jesus Christ, the Glorious One" (2:1 AT).

While the intertextuality of Acts 15:13–21 and James 2:14–26 is illuminating in several ways, especially in light of the *Wirkungsgeschichte* of James since Luther, we draw attention to one conclusion of particular importance. The James of Acts does not underwrite the church's Jewish legacy, whether to abstain from handling meat sacrificed to idols (Acts 15:20, 29; 21:25) or to maintain Mosaic definitions of purity (15:21; 21:21–26), as a *substitute* for repentance, which remains in Acts the defining marker of Christian conversion (15:14, 19; see 2:38). For the missions of Peter and John, Paul and James, "there is salvation in no one else, for there is no other name [= "Jesus Christ of Nazareth, . . . whom God raised from the dead," 4:10] under heaven given among mortals by which we must [= "the *dei* of divine necessity"] be saved" (4:12).[21] For this reason, James introduces his brief to Antioch by arguing that those who have promoted a different gospel in Antioch (see Acts 15:1) did so without his permission (v. 24). Rather, the preservation of the community's Jewish legacy protects the integrity of the Christian mission, of Christian fellowship, and of the Christian gospel proclaimed by Paul among non-Jews.

We think this biblical case is analogous to the relationship between the Pauline and Catholic collections within the New Testament.[22] Simply put, the theological grammars of these collections, one of which is concentrated by the missionary's call for the unbeliever's faith in Jesus and the other by the pastor's exhortation for the believer's faithful works, form a theological whole. Especially when their intracanonical dialogue is introduced and contextualized by Acts, the performance of covenant-keeping works does not displace the profession of faith as heaven's currency, nor is the "obedience of faith" viewed as the progenitor of the "obedience of works." A prior profession of faith in Jesus is presumed by the canonical James (Acts 15:13; James 2:14): he addresses believers, not sinners; communicants, not outsiders. Brought to sharper focus by Acts, then, James 2:14–26 advocates a variety of Christian existence characterized by the interpenetration of faith and works. When the performance of Scripture's rule of life is replaced by pious professions of orthodox faith alone (1:25–27; 2:16, 18–20), faith itself remains incomplete and insufficient

21. Modern scholars of Acts often refer to the narrative's strategic use of "must" (*dei*) as "the *dei* of divine necessity." The theological intention of the storyteller's use of *dei* is to signal to readers that the narrated event and quoted/alluded scripture give clear witness to the outworking of God's plan of salvation within history. Cf. Talbert, *Reading Acts*, 13–14.

22. In particular, see Wall, "Reading Paul with Acts."

(2:22). Such faith fails to square with "the faith of our Lord Jesus Christ" (2:1 AT), whose allegiance to God was demonstrated by his impartial ministry among the poor (1:26–2:1).

Even though the Pauline witness makes clear that public professions of faith are necessary for salvation (so Rom. 10:9), James avers that such professions of faith are insufficient responses to the lordship of Christ unless made complete by the covenant-keeping practices of a "religion that is pure and undefiled before God" (James 1:27; see also 2:8). Cued by James's reading of Abraham's exemplary witness as summarized in 2:22, we might put it this way: The obedience of "faith" demanded by the canonical Paul "is completed by works" (AT) encouraged by the canonical James. Each inspired witness is required in turn to form a whole truth, for friendship with God requires nothing other than a robust faith made whole by faithful works.

We propose a "catholicity of texts," then, in which every biblical witness, Old Testament and New Testament, is picked up and read as an integral part of God's word, the whole of which constitutes a more effective witness to Jesus Christ in today's world than any sum of its various canonized parts. By this we have in mind the dynamic quality that the actual practice of this diversity of texts anticipates when these texts are used to form and guide the membership of the church catholic in the ways of God. For this reason, we strongly encourage the ordered reading of Scripture, exemplified by the lectionary, in which lessons from Old Testament and New Testament are read together as God's word for God's people. By doing so we can imagine the congregations that may benefit from an increased use of the Catholic Epistles (e.g., James 2:1–8; 1 Pet. 2:18–3:7; 1 John 2:3–6) and of the Prophets in worship, instruction, and mission to bring balance in their social practices and theological beliefs wherever the selective and misguided use of the Pauline witness shapes a membership inclined toward *sola fideism*, to the neglect of a radical and risky love for their poor and powerless neighbors.

In a similar way, we also imagine those congregational settings where the volume of Scripture's Pauline witness should be turned up as a check and balance to the selective and misguided use of Gospel traditions. This corrective move seems especially important when discipleship is shaped by a moralistic religion of good works detached from the Spirit's sanctifying operations mediated through the congregation's active practice of Scripture. The reduction or neglect of any part of this biblical whole subverts the church's recognition of the Spirit's intention that every scripture is used to form every member of the church catholic into a whole person who knows and loves God perfectly.

Concluding Thoughts

How then does the church-Scripture analogy play out in terms of catholicity? What is the payoff of analogical reflection relative to this mark? The gains to be made from this exercise relate to the need to keep at bay reductions of the fullness that both the church and Scripture can offer as instruments that the Holy Trinity uses to chasten, invigorate, and empower Christian witness. All too often Christians simply settle in terms of what they believe Christianity to mean and what Scripture says. A status quo sets in, and certain themes, arrangements, or texts become disproportionately highlighted over and against others. But there is something to be said for the fullness of the church's witness across the globe, and analogously, the fullness of Scripture across its many pages. God uses *all* the church's people and *all* of Scripture's texts to refine, chasten, renew, and empower Christian witness today. Of course, temptations for reductions and impoverishments abound, but these need not be heeded. In fact, it is essential that they not be heeded since the integrity and splendor of the Christian way of life stands in the balance.

6

Apostolicity

One could say that each of the marks considered so far is controversial in its own way. Claiming that the church and Scripture are one, holy, and catholic flies against detectable evidence as well as conventional thought. The claim that the church and Scripture are apostolic is no different, although some may find the term unclear. Certainly, some traditions speak in terms of "apostolic succession" to describe their church leadership over time, but outside of these traditions and this usage, what does the church's "apostolicity" signify? What is its importance, especially in relation to the people of God at large and their Scripture?

A quote from the *Catechism of the Catholic Church* shows both the interconnectedness of apostolicity with the other marks as well as some of its dimensions: "What are these bonds of unity? Above all, charity 'binds everything together in perfect harmony.' But the unity of the pilgrim Church is also assured by visible bonds of communion: profession of one faith received from the Apostles; common celebration of divine worship, especially of the sacraments; apostolic succession through the sacrament of Holy Orders, maintaining the fraternal concord of God's family."[1] Most non-Catholic Christians

---

1. *Catechism of the Catholic Church*, §815 (234).

would take exception to the last of these points and related claims made in the *Catechism*;[2] but the first two points stand. As these points indicate through the claims of "*received* from the Apostles" and the "*common* celebration of divine worship," the identity of both the church and its Scripture pivots on claims related to receptivity and sharing. The community of the faithful continues as a transgenerational institution, given that it passes along and shares what it has received to subsequent generations; similarly, the Bible we hold in our hands today has been given to us by those who have preserved it over the centuries, often at painstaking cost. Scripture is something given and received, and its prominence is largely due to preservation and sharing. Such points mark the identities of the church and Scripture as well as their respective purposes and *teloi*.

Practical and Dogmatic Considerations

Apostolicity Is Not Restorationism

A recent documentary on the life of Gore Vidal is subtitled "The United States of Amnesia." The phrase is appropriate in connection with this "secular prophet" and his long-standing witness, one that constantly pressed the country to stay true to its ideals and claims, despite its practices. This peculiar phrase speaks to a condition that we have often noticed in our own work as educators: those in our immediate context within the United States have a fixation on the immediate and the proximate, and as such, the past is readily dismissed or neglected. Although some may blame this condition on youthfulness, one could say that it is a cultural malady all too prone to manifest itself at critical junctures in our shared experience. Americans, after all, are fixated on progress, invention, and competition. Each of these can and is pursued with a kind of valorization of temporality. Perhaps such is the fate of a country with such a young past, although much should not be made of that point since the past that is available is so poorly recalled.

2. We are thinking here particularly of *Catechism of the Catholic Church*, §1400 (392), which highlights the "ecclesial communities derived from the Reformation."

But the matters before us are not simply American or even Western, for they also point to religious impulses, formations, and vices that tend to show up in connection with Protestantism. Taken broadly, the movement of Protestantism often reflects amnesiac properties. Given Protestantism's construction of authority and identity, it is easy to see why this is so. Often what is lifted up as essential within the Protestant spirit is the authority of the Bible and the role of an individual's conscience in ascertaining what is in the Bible. With this dynamic on the table, Protestants have always been prone to divide, and this they have done from their very beginnings. Some have tried to label this dynamic and its operations and effects. Calling it the "Protestant Principle," for example, highlights the tendency to critique and reform human institutions.[3] Protestants, likewise, have sometimes been inclined to think that the best way forward amid perceived stagnancy or tensions is to retain something of the past—typically the biblical witness—but largely as a strategy to secure something urgent, pressing, and thus "new." These and other factors contribute to the possibility of phenomena like denominations of various kinds, "Bible churches" or nondenominational churches, and sundry movements and start-ups that assume their authority with the Bible, on the one hand, and the pressing conditions of a given situation, on the other.

With these tendencies at work, the appeal to apostolicity is peculiar. If the claim is made at all, what is the referent and the rationale for such a move? The referent, of course, is obvious: the apostles who witnessed the incarnate Son and experienced firsthand God's promised salvation through him (see Col. 2:9–10). What we have of their witness is largely in terms of Scripture, so that one could go on and make the move to say that to be apostolic is to be scriptural. The difficulty here is that the apostles, their witness, and their work collectively involve more than simply the New Testament. Yet for Protestants, given the way they typically understand the church, the New Testament is largely all that "is left" of the apostolic witness. What this tends to produce is a kind of "Protestant dilemma," in which the virtues that were appropriate for the Reformation era become, over

3. The phrase is typically associated with Paul Tillich; see his *Protestant Era*.

time and through extensive usage, vices in different contexts (including potentially our own). These vices ultimately serve Protestantism's undoing in that they destabilize or delegitimize forms of communal bonds that are essential in sustaining religious life over time.[4]

One result of these tendencies is a void that in turn funds the call to "return to the fundamentals." There are different ways of characterizing this void and the strategies to fill it. We will focus our attention on one particular word and approach, what we are broadly calling "restorationism." The term has been used in a specific way to demarcate impulses within American revivalism that would depict the source of renewal as a reacquaintance with original artifacts, typically the Bible. Although our use of the term could include specific people and denominations, the impulse is generalizable to more than these since the American religious landscape is drastically marked by the tendency among various Christians to begin anew structurally and institutionally as they recommit themselves to the "golden oldies."

Fascinating in all of this is the irony that as the past is appealed to in a strategic and somewhat nostalgic way (that is, in terms of "the basics," with no subsequent adulterations allowed), a kind of institutional innovation is required for the maintenance of whatever is reclaimed. In other words, the rhetorical appeal is made to the "old" and trustworthy things, but that appeal can only be made within social arrangements that themselves have to be formulated and so are "new." Therefore the gesture is not simply a historicizing or contextualizing kind of endeavor; rather, it also serves as a kind of legitimating mechanism for a specific strategy toward renewal or reform, which in turn requires more than the appeal itself in order to get off the ground. It is no wonder, then, that restorationism of this kind can only multiply church and parachurch divisions. All the while, in these selective appeals to the past, a kind of amnesia is at work as the presence and work of God in wider settings is either ignored or denounced. Thus a kind of institutional innovation often replaces the recognition of the faithfulness of God to God's purposes across time and space.

Neither an appeal to the apostles nor a claim of apostolicity can take the form of a restorationist endeavor without sacrificing key

---

4. For more on this, see Schlabach, *Unlearning Protestantism*.

features of Christian forms of life along the way. One of the reasons for this is that the subsequent innovation that is required to sustain the restoration will depend on wider social arrangements, assumptions, and worldviews that in turn will typically run counter to long-standing Christian arrangements, assumptions, and worldviews, and as such undermine the latter. Perhaps some of that undermining is important as a reform initiative. And yet this process can also be taken to an extreme by delegitimating or ignoring important things as well. Negative examples might include certain kinds of sacramental practice (including regular partaking of the Eucharist); regard for the episcopacy; recognition of monasteries, abbeys, religious orders, and other forms of religious life; and so on.

In contrast to a regard for such constituents of a Christian heritage, the snare of what is contemporaneously trendy and popular can overdetermine "new" institutional efforts. In the modern West, in which the state and the market drive the formation of desire in such totalizing ways, the innovations that result in this context will often reflect such forces. It is no surprise, then, that when people "shop around for a church," the church that they eventually find appealing often already reflects their politics, their racial-ethnic identities, their class, and so on. Within such arrangements, appeal to the apostles can be simply a rhetorical strategy to retain cultural and societal hegemonies. Clearly, if such is the case, the witness of the apostles is being used and manipulated for something other than their own integral witness.

Apostolicity Understood Theologically

If apostolicity is not to be confused with various forms of restorationism as we have considered the term in general, then what is it? Ultimately, apostolicity refers to the undying witness of the triune God in and through human media. The apostles were witnesses of the incarnate God who were given the promise of not being left alone but being accompanied by this same God unto the ends of the earth. For this reason, the church's apostolicity, like all the other marks considered in this volume, is a function of the economic Trinity at work in accomplishing the healing and sanctification of the world.

Apostolicity in particular highlights the need for followers of Jesus to stand in continuity with that work through receiving and sharing in it.

As impactful as this work is in terms of its representation in the New Testament, it is not simply ascertained textually. Apostolicity is not something registered in the Bible that in turn needs to be appropriated in a textual way (that is, by reading, rehearsing, and memorizing portions of text), for it has to do with the culture or ethos of the Christian community, which is inhabited and animated by the presence of the living God.[5] While it is true that part of that culture involves the reading and use of texts, that is only one part. Other parts include communal practices, the collective stratification of time, the highlighting of models for the community to imitate, values and goals that the community aspires to inculcate and achieve, and so on. Perhaps this broader understanding of apostolicity is what motivated some of the restorationists early on, but their accompanying vision often necessarily fell short. Why?

One of the most difficult features of a typical restorationist scheme is that it operates out of a shortsighted vision of the operations of the triune God. Although one extreme of an expansive view of this work would allow that Father, Son, and Holy Spirit could be active anywhere and do anything, another extreme, one that takes a reductive view of this work, would allow that the Trinity's work was preeminently on display in the first century or two of the early church and was minimal thereafter (for whatever reason). This reading of God's activity is not just reductionist but simply wrongheaded. Certainly over time things have changed in terms of Christianity's ethos as well as its place within the world, and yet God's commitment to the church and world is resolutely and uncompromisingly constant. Jesus's promise at the end of the Gospel of Matthew is an apostolic promise, meaning it is not just for his original hearers but also for those who succeed them across time: "And remember, I am with you always, to the end of the age" (28:20). The idealization of the apostles' witness of the incarnate One has its points of truth: the witness of that particular experience is unique. However, that uniqueness in no way creates conditions for inferior experiences by those who follow

5. I am indebted to Flett, *Apostolicity*, for this view.

the apostles across time. Quite the contrary, one could say that belief in such conditions is unique itself, a state of blessedness if you will, as Jesus's response to Thomas seems to indicate: "Have you believed because you have seen me? Blessed are those who have not seen and yet have come to believe" (John 20:29).

The basis of possibility for belief during a post-apostolic age is the ongoing self-presentation of the triune God. The presence and work of God is what maintains continuity between apostolic and post-apostolic eras; it is what constitutes apostolicity, what makes for the true and proper ethos or culture of a professing and believing community. "For where two or three are gathered in my name, I am there among them" (Matt. 18:20). This self-presentation on the part of the triune God does not necessarily and exclusively take place in rapturous, hard-to-pin-down moments of religious experience. We would not dismiss such possibilities in an outright manner, but we are inclined to think that more typical forms of this self-presentation involve synergistic displays of God working through humans in the complexities and challenges of human living.

The patterns of this self-presentation are registered in the incarnation and life of Jesus, a heritage that the apostles have shared and we gratefully receive and recall. This witness has it that this One, after reading Isaiah 61 in the synagogue—"The Spirit of the Lord is upon me, because he has anointed me to bring good news to the poor. He has sent me to proclaim release to the captives and recovery of sight to the blind, to let the oppressed go free, to proclaim the year of the Lord's favor" (Luke 4:18–19)—goes on to say, "Today this scripture has been fulfilled in your hearing" (v. 21). The ongoing ministry of Jesus, as attested by the fourfold Gospel testimony, confirms this fulfillment. Jesus, anointed and animated by the Holy Spirit, challenged the religious establishment of his day for being precisely that: a kind of establishment that was more insulated than generous, more preservationist than apostolic—that is, more for itself than for others. A passage such as this one shows that from the christological and pneumatological depths of God's triune life come gestures in favor of the most needy and vulnerable of our world. Conventionalities and the status quo are turned on their head as a result of God's manifest presence and work. When theologians claim that the economic Trinity is God "for us" (*pro nobis*), this is truly an apostolic claim since it suggests that God reaches out and moves beyond Godself to attend to brokenness and need. Such is God's self-presentation throughout Holy Scripture; it is a distinctive feature of God's character as God works in the world.

Living the Apostolic Way of Life

Many know that the roots of the word "church" suggest the meaning of being "called out."[6] The idea here, it is said, is that the church is made up of those who are "called out" of the world. But that is only one movement, for if the movement would stop here, the church would officially be in the domain of establishment thinking and insularity. The gesture of calling out can only make sense when accompanied with a "sending back," a notion that is at the etymological root of the term "apostolicity" (*apostellō* means "to send"). One sees this double dynamic in Jesus's own interactions with his disciples. When Jesus first "called out" Simon Peter and Andrew, they were fishing, and Jesus greeted them not only with a call but also with a nascent charge: "Follow me, and I will make you fish for people" (Matt. 4:19). This dynamic is registered in the Son's own life, which is sometimes depicted—with echoes of the kenotic hymn of Philippians 2:5–11—in terms of an *exitus-reditus* ("exit-return") scheme.[7]

The church's culture, its ethos, is to be characterized by its collective witness to the work of the triune God, both textually as preserved in Sacred Scripture and practically as displayed in its common life. This is a heritage to be recalled, received, and shared. When the church is conforming itself to the character of God's self-presentation, it is standing in continuity with God's work and as such is living into its apostolic way of life. In this arrangement, the gospel is tangible, observable, documentable, and truly communicable. It spans across eras and contexts, and it is available in the world as a sign of God's grace. We are convinced that nothing more is needed in this world

6. *Ekklēsia*, the Greek word for "church" or "assembly," is formed from *ek* (out, from) + *kaleō* (to call).

7. This is largely a medieval construct, one detectable, for instance, in Thomas Aquinas and his work in the *Summa Theologiae*.

than a church that stands in continuity with the work the Trinity has been doing from the foundation of the world. In a world that periodically asks, "If the Christian God is real, what difference does this belief make?" our response is that the difference can be seen among those communities that stand and live into the apostolic witness to the living, active God. Their works are indicative of God's works; their life is indicative of God's life; their love is indicative of God's love.

The continuity at work here is quite radical. The synergism is difficult to predetermine since from one perspective God works through human agents to accomplish God's purposes, yet from another perspective, as human agents participate in God's work, they render that work in some sense unto God as acts of worship. Such are the implications of Matthew 25: In relation to the hungry, the thirsty, the stranger, the naked, the sick, and the prisoner, the operative understanding is that when these are cared for and ministered to, Christ himself is cared for and ministered to: "Truly I tell you, just as you did it to one of the least of these who are members of my family, you did it to me" (Matt. 25:40). Such is the culture of the church and the mark of its apostolicity—toiling in the economy of God's creation so that there is a visible and detectable witness of God's presence working to heal and to mend.

The Church-Scripture Analogy

The church catholic's theological agreements and unifying grammar are forged by the gospel of the apostles. Their pluriform eyewitness of the historical Jesus supplies the single referent of biblical interpretation, which yields both the normative content of Christian proclamation to the nations (see Luke 24:44–49) and the practical criterion of the community's covenant-keeping koinōnia with God (see 1 John 1:1–4). As Brevard Childs puts it, "Apostolicity became a dynamic term to encompass historical, substantive, functional, and personal qualities of the most basic core of the faith."[8] We contend that the church's affirmation of its apostolic identity is secured by

8. Childs, *Church's Guide for Reading Paul*, 21.

the faithful practice of Scripture in worship, catechesis, mission, and personal devotions, since Scripture endures as the principal carrier of the apostolic witness to the incarnate One.

Moreover, Scripture's biography of the apostles, retrieved from the fourfold Gospel and especially from Acts, portrays them as moral and spiritual exemplars; their canonized memory stipulates a pattern of life and faithfulness that continues to define the church's public life in the world. It may even be true that the apostles demonstrate how to receive, rely upon, and read the synagogue's scripture through a christological lens as an essential witness to the redemptive ways of God.

In both these senses, theological and moral, the apostles of the church are presented as Spirit-filled witnesses of the divine word, proclaimed and embodied. The faith community that self-identifies with the canonical portraits is like-minded: It too is a prophetic carrier of God's word to the world and publicly testifies to the effects of God's saving grace by sharing its possessions with the needy (Acts 2:42–47; see Gal. 2:10). It too is a priestly advocate who embraces the marginal and heals the sick (Acts 5:12–16; see James 5:1–6, 13–16). By engaging in these ministries, it too boldly announces the apocalypse of God's salvation (Acts 4:19–31; cf. Rom. 1:16–18), which turns the world upside down (Acts 17:1–6; see 1 Cor. 1:18–31). Simply put, the apostolic mark underscores the continuity between the beliefs and practices of a Christian congregation and those of the risen Lord's apostles, whom he chose, gifted, and appointed to lead the messianic community in his absence. Analogous to this claim, then, is a claim about Scripture's apostolic mark: it is the sanctified depository of the gospel of the apostles whom the Spirit chose, gifted, and appointed to form a people whose successive generations do and say what the risen Lord and his apostles have begun (see Acts 1:1–2).

If these claims about apostolicity frame Scripture's analogical relationship with the church, two caveats are added as cautionary notes in reading the following exposition. First, the apostles' eyewitness of God's revelation personified by the historical Jesus allowed an unmediated access to the truth about God that the church does not enjoy. Their appointment as Spirit-filled carriers of God's word privileged them within the divine economy—a privilege Paul recognized when he greeted Titus (Titus 1:1–3). We claim nothing more about this real difference between the apostles and the apostolic church and its Scripture than this: the church is not a community of apostles but of Christ's disciples who continue to learn from the canonical deposit of memories and texts the Spirit has sanctified for the church's continuing use.

In fact, Scripture's appointment as a sacred auxiliary of the Holy Spirit in reliably communicating God's word to God's people must presume a substantive continuity—an "apostolic succession"—between what the apostles heard and saw of the incarnate One and the effectiveness of this historical memory preserved by Scripture in bringing readers into a saving relationship with the triune God. The point is simply this: the eyewitness of the apostles testifies to an experience—a personal presence—that the church no longer has.

But neither is the analogical relationship between the two claimed "in spite of" this qualitative difference between an unmediated and mediated reception of divine revelation. We recognize that the Spirit has used the distinctive contributions of different media and messengers during different moments of salvation's history to accomplish God's single redemptive plan. In this case, the holy ends of the apostolic eyewitness and the apostolic church and its Scripture are the same, if also perfectly suited to a particular moment in time. This too is an aspect of divine providence according to which God appoints and orders every witness to God's word and work, whether mediated or unmediated, to align with this common end: "the self-presentation of the triune God, the free work of sovereign mercy in which God wills, establishes and perfects saving fellowship with himself in which humankind comes to know, love and fear God above all things."[9]

A second caveat to bear in mind is that, even though the following exposition depends on a New Testament depiction of an apostolic witness to construct the analogical relationship between the church's self-identity as an apostolic community and Scripture as an apostolic text, we recognize and elevate the interpretive necessity of approaching the church's Scripture as a two-Testament witness. Paul writes that the church "has been constructed on a foundation of the apostles

9. Webster, *Holy Scripture*, 13.

and the prophets, with Christ Jesus himself as the cornerstone" (Eph. 2:20 AT). The church's confession of itself as an apostolic community does not grant permission to exclude or minimize the gospels of the prophets as part of the witness to God's redemptive work because of Christ.

Scripture as Witness to the Risen Jesus

While the nature of the working relationship between the two Testaments remains contested, we simply claim at the outset that the unmediated access of the prophets to Israel's God through theophany and divine speech is in some sense repeated, if also made clearer, by the unmediated access of the apostles to the historical Jesus. The prophets' reception of the divine word and the apostles' eyewitness of the incarnate word are of a single piece.

On this basis, the risen Lord, in his hermeneutics of Scripture, asserts himself as the single referent of the gospels of the Old Testament prophets, a christological meaning that requires the use of figural or typological readings to retrieve. However, we are convinced, in light of what we have already said, that other meanings are derived from reading Old Testament texts according to their address in the history of Israel. The church receives the Old Testament as a discrete and distinctive witness to the God who is incarnate in Jesus and witnessed by his apostles. Any historical investigation that targets theological understanding is constrained by a purposeful desire to know the Old Testament witness to Israel's God and God's way of saving Israel, for it is this God who promises to restore and bless Israel and who frames and freights what the apostles see and hear in Jesus.[10]

There is no more arresting example of the dynamic nature of this christological hermeneutics of Scripture than the Letter to the Hebrews. Though the writer introduces a "word of exhortation" (13:22) by comparing God's past and partial revelation to Israel's prophets

10. F. A. Spina nicely captures one sense of Jesus's hermeneutics of Scripture, arguing that a reading of the Old Testament story of Israel as Christian Scripture requires "seeing Israel—*canonical* Israel—as a figure for the church." Spina, "Israel as a Figure for the Church," 3 (emphasis original), see also 11–22.

(1:1) with God's present and final revelation in the Son (1:2),[11] the extensive use of Israel's scripture makes it clear that Scripture's prophetic witness to God's way of salvation is *not* superseded by the apostolic witness of the Son (2:3). In fact, Israel's scripture continues to vocalize the eternal and penetrating words of the triune God (4:12) and the Son (2:12–13; 10:5), not only as the definitive witness to Jesus's own redemptive role within the divine economy *in advance of* his messianic work as Jesus of Nazareth but also as the normative guide in the church's reception of the apostolic proclamation of him (2:1–4; cf. Gal. 3:24). William Faulkner's memorable line from *Requiem for a Nun* comes to mind: "The past is never dead. It's not even past."

Scripture's apostolic mark is not a historical matter settled by criticism's unsettling investigation into the authorship of biblical writings—that is, whether they were written by an apostle and then claimed the apostolic mark on this basis. Rather, apostolicity is a *theological* category that grants special authority to the witnesses of those "apostles whom [Jesus] had chosen" to continue all that Jesus "did and taught from the beginning" (Acts 1:1–2). They were not only eyewitnesses of the historical Jesus (cf. Acts 1:21–22) but had experienced through him the salvation God promised according to Israel's scripture (cf. Acts 10:38–39, 43). The church's purposeful collection and canonization of apostolic writings in forming the New Testament necessarily coheres to the theological content of this apostolic witness to their encounter and experience of the risen Jesus.

---

11. Cf. Griffiths, *Hebrews and Divine Speech*, esp. 49–61. Griffiths's reading of the letter's opening exordium (1:1–4) focuses on two different roles denoted by the preposition *en* (+ dative) in the writer's parallel claims about the continuity and contrast of divine speech in the economy of divine revelation. Each prepositional phrase envisages a different genre of divine revelation. On the one hand, God spoke in the past (old covenant) "through" (*en* of agency) the prophets (1:1), which Griffiths extends to include its angelic delivery system in 1:4–2:4. On the other hand, this same God has spoken again "in these last days" (new covenant) "in" (*en* of location) a Son (1:2) whose nature and performances are divine (1:2–3). Griffiths contends that the inherent superiority of the Son when compared to the angels regards the rhetorical quality of the incarnation as a medium of the divine word: eyewitnesses can hear and attest to him, and then declare (2:3) with credibility his message of salvation (2:2). Further, God can add God's own historical testimony to this eyewitness message, which presumably occurred at Pentecost (2:4). Against Griffiths, we think it plausible to identify these eyewitnesses with the apostolic witness.

Critically, the church's appropriation of these apostolic writings must also cohere in some sense to this same theological content if what Jesus began is to continue into our own day and social worlds.

In previous chapters we have mentioned the extraordinary purchase of Luke's version of the risen Jesus's Great Commission (24:44–49). Prior to his final speech, Jesus "opens the minds" of his apostles to a normative hermeneutics of Israel's scripture, which identifies his messianic mission and its redemptive effects as its referent. The antecedent of the commission proper, in which Jesus asserts, "You are witnesses [μάρτυρες, *martyres*] of these things" (v. 48), includes both his messianic life and a particular way of reading Scripture that interprets it rightly for the nations. While the history of interpreting Israel's scripture in the synagogue and the church makes other meanings of these holy texts, according to Jesus their principal use is to support the eyewitness testimony of his apostles.

Before considering the realization of Jesus's directive in Acts, consider how the final two uses of the verbal form of "witness" (μαρτυρέω, *martyreō*) in the Fourth Gospel frame for readers what is at stake by an apostolic eyewitness. According to the narrator's sidebar in John 19:35, the one (presumably the apostle John) who "saw" the soldier thrust his spear into Jesus's side, and saw the blood and water that came out (v. 34), "has witnessed" it, "knows" it, and "tells the truth" about it. The density of epistemic catchwords used by the narrator underscores its apologetic or forensic value. The immediate effect of apostolic testimony to the messianic event is to presume its factual reliability against any who think it false or misleading. In particular, when the proclamation of the gospel needs to persuade an unbelieving or even hostile audience, the appeal to an eyewitness account of the historical Jesus's suffering and resurrection is critical.

Moreover, the narrator extends the factual truth of the apostle's eyewitness to explain that what happened fulfills Scripture (vv. 36–37). Consistent with Jesus's hermeneutics of Scripture according to Luke, then, the Fourth Gospel confirms that what the apostle sees agrees with a messianic reading of Scripture. Readers should expect to find this same theo-logic ordering the narrative of the *missio Dei* that follows in Acts. Significantly, on this basis the narrator supplies the intention of this editorial comment for readers in a characteristically

Johannine idiom: "so that you [readers] may also believe" (v. 35 AT). While the curious addition of "also" (καί, *kai*) targets the readers, it doubtless is self-referential: What he has seen and heard of Jesus has made him a believer. His is the reliable testimony of a convinced follower. This platitude is picked up again to state the purpose of the entire Gospel in 20:30–31, which founds the veracity of its story of Jesus on the apostle's eyewitness.

The Fourth Evangelist's final use of μαρτυρέω (21:24) ends his Gospel. While the purpose and meaning of this text remain contested, it clearly echoes and we think repeats the main point scored by John 19:35 (see above). But its setting in the Gospel's epilogue changes its force. In this instance, the narrator has the "beloved disciple" in mind (see 21:20–23). This use of μαρτυρέω, then, glosses the identity of the apostle himself, since the identity of the testifier cannot be detached from the written testimony itself: the one who "witnesses these things" is the one who has "written these things" (AT). This signal disciple of the Fourth Gospel is the personification of the canonical apostle.

His persona is implied by the various allusions to "the beloved disciple" in the Fourth Gospel. The figure who emerges is not so much recognized by his virtuous character as by his intimate placement with and experience of the historical Jesus. This canonical apostle is the ultimate insider and so the most reliable witness who can testify to things to which no one else has access. He is the one reclining next to Jesus when he predicts his betrayal (13:23); he alone stands next to Mary beside the cross when Jesus dies (19:26); he is the first to the tomb to see it empty and so to believe the resurrection (20:2, 4, 8–9); he is the first to recognize the risen Lord by the sea of Tiberias (21:7); and he is the one about whom the risen Jesus issues his final (and ambiguous) saying in the Gospel (v. 22). It is on the epistemic basis of this intimate knowing that the narrator can finally say, "We know that his testimony is true" (v. 24).

John's epilogue functions as the apt conclusion to the fourfold Gospel since it paves a gateway into the Acts narrative, in which the apostles fulfill Jesus's prophecy that they "will be my witnesses [μάρτυρες] . . . to the end of the earth" (Acts 1:8 AT). They are witnesses in the manner of John's "beloved disciple," whose insider status provides reliable information about Jesus to proclaim to others. Acts emphasizes more than John that the apostolic witness of the risen One is both enabled by the Spirit and confirmed—even scripted—by Scripture's witness as a mutually glossing whole. The adumbration of μάρτυρες in Acts illustrates this point.

According to the initial use of μάρτυρες in Acts 1:8, widely acknowledged as the storyteller's road map to help readers navigate his narrative world, those chosen as Jesus's apostolic successors (v. 2) are promised the Holy Spirit's power as the marker and means of their vocation as witnesses of the risen Jesus. The criterion of membership in this apostolate is clarified by the selection of Matthias, who is not only a witness to the resurrection (v. 22) but also a participant in the community of disciples that traveled with the historical Jesus throughout his messianic career (v. 21; see 1 John 1:1–3). An intimate, comprehensive memory of the life of Jesus is required to give a reliable witness to him to the "end of the earth"—the essential feature of John's canonical Gospel.

The location of Matthias's story in the narrative introduction suggests its importance to the plotline. Given the controversial nature of Paul's apostleship, which probably was due to a résumé that lacked this very attribute (e.g., Gal. 1:10–2:14; 2 Cor. 11:1–12:21), his story in Acts may be read as an apologia for his enduring ecclesial authority. In fact, the canonical Paul of Acts seems to recognize this problem in his rehearsal of the church's origins when he speaks of the apostles as "witnesses" of the historical Jesus in a way that excludes himself (Acts 13:31). With this problem on the table, then, Luke's story of Paul's mission as the personification of faithful Israel's vocation as "a light to the nations" (v. 47 AT; see Isa. 49:6 LXX) unfolds as an apologia of his importance for the church's future based on a different but equally satisfying epistemic attribute: his revelatory experiences of the risen Jesus, which include repeated testimony to his apostle-like commission (Acts 9:15–16; 22:12–16; 26:15–18) and sustained continuity with the Twelve in both the kerygmatic content of his missionary speeches and the conflict and Spirit-empowered "signs and wonders" they occasioned (5:12; 15:12). After all, it is Paul who arrives in Rome, "the end of the earth" in this narrative world, to announce the "kingdom of God" (28:30–31; see 1:3) and so fulfill

Jesus's prophecy about his witnesses that begins and freights this canonical story (1:8).

Two other repetitions of μάρτυρες in Acts are mentioned to fill out our profile. Virtually all commentators recognize that its successive uses by Peter in his initial (and so programmatic) apostolic proclamations of the gospel (Acts 2:32; 3:15) serve an apologetic purpose, and effectively so, since they help to ready his Jewish audience to respond to the call to repent and turn to Christ (2:38; 3:19). Significantly for our purpose, Peter claims his status as eyewitness of the risen Jesus to underwrite his messianic reading of the scripture he cites or echoes that, he claims, scripts God's "definitive plan" of salvation (2:23 AT), which God "foretold by the utterances of all the prophets" (3:18 AT). In his missionary speeches Peter's appropriation of Scripture as a textual witness to the risen Jesus is of a piece both in content and function with his eyewitness of the same.

Curiously, it is not the apostle Peter of Acts whose appeal to Scripture confirms his own experience of God's inclusion of uncircumcised Gentiles in the covenant community (thereby overturning Gen. 17) but rather the nonapostle James, the brother of Jesus (see Acts 15:13–21). Nonetheless, their exchange at the pivotal Jerusalem Council suggests a working relationship between Scripture and apostolic testimony according to which the normativity of Peter's eyewitness of Cornelius's salvation is affirmed and extended by James's midrash of Amos 9:11–12 (LXX).

The second noteworthy use of μάρτυρες is the apostles' stunning declaration that their own eyewitness to "these things" about Jesus is also of a piece with the discrete witness of the Holy Spirit (Acts 5:32). We should notice that "these things" correspond to the core beliefs about Jesus that he has opened their minds to know from Scripture and commissioned them to proclaim to the nations (see Luke 24:46–47). Jesus has promised them that the acuity and ability to do so effectively will be enabled by the Spirit's "power" (see Luke 24:49; Acts 1:8). But this use of μάρτυρες to include the Spirit implies that the Spirit's power is not some impersonal force of supernature that merely enhances or calls to mind what the apostles have already learned from watching and listening to Jesus. Nor does the exercise of the Spirit prove to be the providential glue that holds together the church's two principal witnesses: (1) Scripture's witness, which the Spirit brings into existence and inspires to allow for its normative interpretation; and (2) the apostolic witness, which consists of the gospel's proclamation that the Spirit empowers and the experience of forgiveness that the Spirit's reception confirms.

In this sense, we do not agree with those who propose that Luke's idea of the Spirit's witness trades on the same tradition that the Fourth Evangelist has used to define the Spirit's presumptive role as divine "witness" to Jesus's discipleship following his departure (John 15:26–27). According to John's narrative, the Spirit inspires the apostles to recall Jesus's teaching to fund their own teaching in order to compensate for Jesus's physical absence from them (see 14:26). The Spirit of Acts bears its own discrete witness to Jesus that agrees with and supports the interpenetrating scriptural and apostolic witness; we should presume that the "power" of the Spirit cues a charismatic dialogue, especially in the various speeches of Acts, which adds to and enables an even more precise and compelling presentation of the gospels of the apostles.

Based on these various observations, we are now prepared to offer the primary elements of a typology that envisions Scripture as a Spirit-inspired witness analogous to the church's apostolic mark. First, Scripture's sanctified performances as a witness are not indicated by literary form; witness is not a literary genre but rather a theological confession. It is self-evident that the various forms of the church's witness to God's saving mercies, which believers affirm are "apostolic" in both content and effect, differ in form from Scripture's textual witness. What our brief study of the idea of witness demonstrates, however, is their common purpose: the continuing witness of both the church and its Scripture is, in all their Spirit-led performances, apostolic in terms of foundational content and formative consequence.

We have argued that the church's postbiblical canonization of its Scripture, a process of spiritual discernment superintended by the Holy Spirit, was initially ordered by the reasoned recognition of the text's apostolicity. Such a recognition was possible only by congregational practice when the actual hearing of these texts in worship and catechesis made clear their agreement with what the apostles had seen and heard of the historical Jesus, the incarnate Son of God. This testimony, of course, predates the canonical process, whether in the memory of the faith communities the apostles founded or in the earliest institutional forms, and was the theological metric used during the canonical process to guarantee the apostolicity of the church's Scripture. In fact, the congregational practice of its apostolic depository formed the spiritual capacity to discern those texts that the Spirit sanctified as Scripture. This includes the church's decision to receive Israel's scripture from the synagogue for its enduring use as a biblical testimony to the incarnate One.

In this sense, the church's recognition of apostolicity (or of apostolic succession) is not primarily a question of authorship. Our judgment, as we have suggested above, is not based on modern criticism's verdict about the real authors (and related prolegomena) of biblical texts, which we think is an intellectual dead end. What the church recognizes by its practice of sacred texts is their theological substance and effectiveness in forming a Christian understanding of and experiences with the living Lord. Weber rightly declares, "The church and all its acts are ostensive, pointing beyond and behind themselves to that which transcends and precedes them. . . . The canonic decision of the Church is essentially its confession of the norm already given it, the standard by which it was prepared to let itself be measured."[12] This "standard," Webster avers, is the apostolic eyewitness and experience of the risen Christ.[13]

Second, our understanding of Scripture's witness is freighted by the apostles' eyewitness of the historical Jesus, the one and only Messiah, whom we confess is the incarnate Son of God. Scripture's authority and holy effects depend on the authority of the holy One to whom it points. Among the most important features of the biblical portrait of the canonical apostle (see above) is the role as an interpreter of what is seen and heard. Any interpretive approach that accords with Jesus's way of reading Scripture, which presumes its singular referent is God (subject) and God's salvation (predicate), recognizes that Scripture is not a self-interpreting book. Scripture's

12. Weber, *Foundations of Dogmatics*, 1:252.
13. Webster, *Holy Scripture*, 64.

witness to God is mediated by testimony that is edited, composed, transcribed, and circulated in the canonical Gospels of the various apostles. Moreover, these Gospels are constituted by a particular way of reading that itself is apostolic in that it agrees with the instruction of Jesus, who opened their minds to retrieve Scripture's normative meaning.

An apostolic interpretation of Scripture does not invalidate other meanings and methods. If Scripture is a sacred text that the Spirit has sanctified for holy ends, then it commends our most careful and reverent attention. Every textual criticism, especially those that analyze the linguistic composition and ecclesial transmission and reception of a particular text, is indispensable for its most effective uses. We also encourage the cultivation of those intellectual virtues, such as honesty and open-minded handling of evidence, that are necessary in the pursuit of what is the gospel truth—the holy end to which the apostolic witness applies (see John 19:35; 21:24).

But at the same time we reject the modern fiction that such an investigation is engaged with benign neutrality. Every interpretation of Scripture is vested with particular bones to pick, whether epistemological, theological, or sociological. The real issue for us is which bones we should pick. Scripture's apostolic mark also marks its faithful readers as those who seek after theological understanding. They seek ends that form in them greater love for God and for all their neighbors. An apostolic interpretation of Scripture is therefore regulated by an apostolic Rule of Faith that consists of theological agreements stipulated by Jesus and by a manner of life that evinces the fruit of the Spirit.

Concluding Thoughts

Apostolicity is a mark made possible by the self-presentation of the Trinity. It speaks to a heritage that is graciously given by God and gratefully received, recalled, and shared by those who seek to be formed into God's character. Given that the term "apostolicity" references practices, texts, and ways of life, it relates to the culture, the ethos, of those who are disciples of Jesus, from the ones first called by Jesus himself to the ones of today. For this reason, apostolicity is appropriate in speaking of the church, a body that is the instantiation of this culture across time and space. The mark is also appropriate in relation to Scripture since it is a textual witness to God's self-presentation: Scripture is ordered and structured so as to contribute to the shape and shaping power of this ethos. All in all, the faithfulness of the earliest apostles through their lives, practices, and writings suggests that we all stand on their shoulders. But such a gift is itself a tribute to God's faithfulness and goodness, suggesting that God never leaves us alone and without a witness to God's steadfast love and care.

7

The Church's Practice of Scripture

The premise of this book is this: how God's people think about Scripture should guide how they practice it in worship, catechesis, mission, and personal devotions. To think theologically about Scripture naturally entails questions of ontology (What is it?) and teleology (What is it for?). The theology of Scripture that undergirds this book highlights the terms "canon" and "means of grace" to secure both its nature as an auxiliary of the Holy Spirit and its holy ends in forming a community of the faithful.

Implicit in this orienting commitment is our observation that nowhere in Scripture do authors of these texts claim they are busy writing "scripture" for their audiences. They are engaged in ordinary acts of communication in which they write stories, letters, prophecies, songs, apocalypses, wisdom sayings, and poems through which the God they worship is witnessed. While modern criticism targets the communicative intentions of these ancient authors for their first audiences, we seek to move this interpretive target forward to a post-biblical setting when the church received and reread these same texts for a new day; by doing so we recognize the illuminating presence of the Spirit, who cued their canonization and continuing use as Scripture. Reading biblical texts as canonical means reading them again and again for each and every new day, but only according to the *church's* communicative intention: to form congregations who know God and who love God and all their neighbors deeply and actively.

If this is so, then it seems logical to us that the Scripture the church formed under the aegis of God's sanctifying Spirit shares the church's nature and vocation. That is, such a community will use Scripture in partnership with God's Spirit to be reshaped in its character into Christlikeness in order to witness to what our loving God continues to do for a lost and needy world. Scripture communicates God's Word to the extent that its interpretation and performance accomplish God's purposes among God's people for the sake of all creation.

We take this assessment of Scripture as normative. In this light, we have sought to expose a way of thinking about Scripture's nature and holy ends that we think is deficient: the Christ-Scripture analogy. We believe it is inadvisable to construct an analogical connection between the affirmation of Christ's two natures, divine and human, and the constitution of Scripture as similarly divine and human. Such an attempt not only diminishes the uniqueness of the incarnation but also considers Scripture's nature as an unhelpful binary that presses affirmations about Scripture to one extreme or another: either it is just another human book or it is a divine book whose words are taken literally as the words of God written down without error (since God cannot lie), even if in the idiom of their human authors. We believe the histories of various fundamentalisms on both sides of this binary, both academic and ecclesial, make this analogy problematic.

We seek to offer readers an alternative: the church-Scripture analogy. Using the marks of the church as confessed in the Nicene Creed as our rubric, we have developed an expansive way of rethinking the ontology and teleology of Scripture. Along the way we have provided reasons that secure this analogy as more suitable than the familiar Christ-Scripture analogy, especially since our core affirmations of the church and Scripture are closer dogmatic analogues. We have developed points of connection often overlooked between systematic studies of ecclesiology and "bibliology."[1] We have also noted limits and even abuses of each. Our replacement analogy does not intend to

---

1. This is the language of Telford Work; see the term's initial definition in *Living and Active*, 8.

end the constructive discourse, especially grounded in the "analogical imagination,"[2] that continues to animate an invigorating reflection of Scripture's nature and role among the faithful.

This last remark raises a significant point. Our argument is not simply about analogy making. Its greater purpose is to guide Christian readers in their approach to Scripture and in their understanding and utilization of it. Analogy making can be one part of this process, but it is only a single strategy. The larger-scale question has to do with the intellectual and spiritual formation of *faithful* readers. In other words, analogy making is an activity that cannot adequately address the whole of what is involved with formation. We are speaking here of the cultivation of intellectual and spiritual virtues, intellectual and spiritual senses, intellectual and spiritual practices. If this species of formation is the holy end toward which the Spirit moves faithful readers, then a sustained, intentional, and directed communal process is needed.

Faithfulness as Cultivating the Interior Life

At every stage of a believer's life, there is always more to experience and grow into as part of the journey of faith. When people come to accept Christ, this is, of course, a joyous occasion. At the same time, this occasion is simply a start: it may mark the end of one process, but it also marks the beginning of a new one. Likewise, those who have been believers for decades are involved in a process: they too are on a journey, one that has been taking place for some time but that by no means is over. The apostle Paul hints at this for his own life: "Beloved, I do not consider that I have made it my own; but this one thing I do: forgetting what lies behind and straining forward to what lies ahead, I press on toward the goal for the prize of the heavenly call of God in Christ Jesus" (Phil. 3:13–14). As Methodists, we are inclined to use the language of salvation and sanctification here, as we have previously. The journey of faith is the "way of salvation," the path of holiness, the process of sanctification.

2. Here we appropriate the seminal phrase of David Tracy to characterize the theologian's ongoing reflection on an ecclesial norm or "classic"—in this case the nature and function of Scripture—in light of new insights about its relationship to God, the church, and the world; see Tracy, *Analogical Imagination*.

The path's goal is what Paul earlier alludes to in his Letter to the Philippians: having the mind of Christ (see 2:5). Conformity to Christ in the power of the Holy Spirit is what Christians are striving for in this life. This is a lifelong process because of not simply the constant threat of sin but also the very constitution of human beings, who are characterized by potential and require discipline and genuine work for that potential to be realized and for their capacities and abilities to be honed and developed. In light of this, sanctification does not simply touch on instantaneous dynamics. More generally and routinely it involves the warp and woof of everyday life, what Latino/a theologians call *lo cotidiano*.

Having the mind of Christ can take on many shapes and expressions. This variety should not remove the need for securing this claim concretely. Christians are often inclined to use very demanding phrases in their discourse (loving God and neighbor, walking according to the Spirit and not the flesh, and so on), but such prominent usage has a way of domesticating and taming these terms, allowing them to stand without their accompanying demands and so to remain abstract and amorphous. Having the mind of Christ sounds fitting and appropriate to Christians, but what can it mean, especially in relation to the reading of Scripture?

We could answer this question in many different ways, but here we stress humility as an orienting disposition and as a spiritual and intellectual virtue that is in need of cultivation by Scripture's readers.[3] For us, humility functions as a master or umbrella formational category, one that we believe is crucial for appreciating Scripture's unity, holiness, catholicity, and apostolicity. Each of the chapters we have devoted to the marks of Scripture has challenged the status quo of how believers may view the church, Scripture, and their interrelationship, yet the recognition of such challenges without defensive reactions requires an abiding sense of humility.

We speak of humility as a spiritual and intellectual virtue because we see it as flourishing similarly to other synergistic dynamics: As we kneel before God in prayer and confession, we are shaped by the

---

3. For a suggestive work on humility, hailing from the realm of systematics, see Pardue, *Mind of Christ*.

Holy One in our midst. In this sense, humility is a work of God in the human heart, a fruit of the transforming work of the Spirit that takes place as believers "practice the presence of God." It is not a virtue in the strict Aristotelian sense but more so within a Thomistic theological framing, one that has resonances with the theme of the affections in the Wesleyan tradition. In another aspect, humility understood in a Christian way is a kind of intellectual virtue, a modus operandi by which disciples pursue their work. Humility characterizes Christian study because Christians recognize knowledge as not simply factual in some generic sense but also as moral. What we know, how we know, and how we learn are all moral activities shaped by shared commitments and goals. Humility is an intellectual virtue for Christians because it demonstrates itself among those who recognize that they only know in part, seeing as if through a mirror dimly (see 1 Cor. 13:12). Whatever is achieved intellectually by Christians is so by the sheer gratuity of God; that orienting concern must ground, characterize, and shape the work that ensues.

Of course, we as Christians have a model expression of humility in the person of Jesus Christ. Paul exhorts the Philippian community to have the mind of Christ at the beginning of what is commonly called the kenotic hymn of Philippians 2:5–11. The hymn itself highlights a movement of humility: nonexploitation, emptying, humbling oneself, obedience, death, and the cross. From the perspective of Paul, having the mind of Christ involves a kind of humility that can build up the church amid tensions and divisions. Given that the church's Scripture-reading practices often lead to many of those divisions, it may be wise to consider humility in this context.

What does a community actively seeking humility in conformity to the mind of Christ and by the power of the Spirit look like in terms of its scriptural engagement?[4] One indicator would be that the community understands its interpretations of Scripture as provisional. As we have already stated in this text, reading Scripture (like reading in general) is interdependent in part on the social imaginary of its faithful readers. People recognize elements in a text and emphasize

---

4. In what follows, we tend to stress the "virtue-in-interpretation" option highlighted in Fowl, "Virtue." For another take on how humility can work among a community of wise readers, see Lim and Castelo, *Hosea*, chap. 15.

and prioritize themes they "see" based significantly on what they have experienced and how they have been shaped.[5] Therefore, in any given moment, a community of readers will read a passage of Scripture based on such contingencies. And, yet, these contingencies change over time. Thus a parable, narrative, principle, or theme of Scripture may be viewed differently by a given community as it learns more about the text and about life generally. A text's meaning is not secured independently of life; quite the contrary, the text comes to have meaning within all of life's vicissitudes and challenges. Provisionality here means that a community can change its interpretation of Scripture over time, based on how that community develops intellectually and spiritually. What we are suggesting is a "soft relativism" (one that accounts for contingencies and contexts) rather than a "hard relativism" (one suggesting that nothing can be secured in terms of meaning and truth claims because contingencies and contexts thoroughly destabilize the interpretive process).

An experience from our own lives can serve as an illustration of such provisionality. Our institutional home, Seattle Pacific University, suffered a campus shooting on June 5, 2014. Many people were traumatized, a few physically shot, and one killed. The person killed was a student of one of us (Castelo). One of the first things our community did after the shooting was to gather for prayer and worship that very same day. During that gathering time, we read passages from Scripture, ones that highlighted the themes of lament and questioning. After that experience, we now read these passages differently. Our appreciation of these portions of Scripture is now deeper in light of this horrible experience and the act of worshiping as a community in its aftermath. We read such passages in one way before this event; we read them in another, deeper way after it. What provisionality here means is that we are always growing and changing with the text so that the text registers itself differently in our lives over time.

Tied to provisionality is corrigibility. Humble readers of Scripture are willing to admit that they could be misdirected in a particular reading or application of Scripture. Those of us who have been in the

5. For a more extensive treatment of this theme, see Westphal, *Whose Community? Which Interpretation?*

church for a long time tend to believe that certain passages just mean certain things rather than others, primarily because we have heard sermons and lessons to that effect. Humble readers of Scripture seek to have the mind of Christ and allow for the possibility that their interpretation of a passage is off-kilter, particularly as they are exposed to a bevy of arguments that take into account a number of plausibly relevant factors (the ancient world of the passage, linguistic analysis, the text surrounding the passage, and so on). Faithful, spiritually mature readers of Scripture will be open to having their minds changed and their viewpoints altered based on fitting and compelling evidence. Jesus expected this of his earliest followers when he remarked, "You have heard that it was said. . . . But I say to you . . ." Jesus was challenging interpretations of Scripture that were misdirected, ones that were often the result of people's self-hardening. To be a follower of Jesus means being willing to have one's interpretations of Scripture changed and corrected.

Corrigibility not only relates to interpretation but also to application as well. Some Christians have used certain passages of Scripture to judge others or to perpetuate practices that are broadly in nonconformity to the gospel message. Whether as justifications for treating women or minorities a certain way, as explanations for why tragedies happen, or something else, Scripture is constantly put to use in ways that are inappropriate and hurtful to the whole people of God. At such moments, Christians must be vigilant to teach and correct one another for the sake of the gospel's embodiment and performance. Therefore, not just the interpretation but also the handling of Scripture reflect and contribute to a community's formation and development.

A third feature of humility that is Christlike when related to the reading of Scripture is dialogue. Scripture is to be contemplated and "chewed on" over time with diverse others, something we highlighted in our discussion of catholicity. As a further example, one of us (Wall) has greatly benefited from reading Scripture over the years with Orthodox Jews. This practice has been extended formally and collectively to the work of others who are engaged in theological interpretations of Scripture, especially the readings that seek to bring the Old Testament and New Testament into conversation as a self-glossing witness to God's redemptive word. On first hearing of such activity, some Christians might wonder about the merits and outcomes. Our response would simply be that the effects and fruits of such exchanges cannot be predetermined or anticipated ahead of time. Scripture itself alludes to "Melchizedek types" throughout its pages, those outside the boundaries of the covenant who yet speak to the covenant people about God's purposes and plans. If such is the case with "outsiders," how much more so is dialogue important among "insiders," those within the covenant who are seeking a word from their God. A hortatory or comforting word from the Lord can come from anyone. The same is true in relation to scriptural insights and applications.[6] To be in genuine dialogue with diverse others about Scripture means that privileges of various kinds must be renounced for the sake of being open to what God may be doing in a particular set of circumstances.

We could mention other intellectual and spiritual virtues besides humility, but we especially want to stress it within this context given the kinds of self-privileging and signs of pridefulness often on display among those who read and apply Scripture. A wise and well-formed community of Scripture's readers will be humble before God and others as they seek to understand and apply Holy Writ. All too often in our experience, it is the pride of Scripture's readers that destroys their charity and intellectual virtuosity.

Practicing Scripture

As we now move to speak more extensively of a faithful congregation's practice of Scripture, it is important to note that our use of the word "practice" is deliberate. Much like athletes or musicians who practice hard to improve their craft, the faithful congregation picks up and

6. One of us (Castelo) had an experience a few years ago that speaks to this point: Among the most important insights I have received from classroom dialogue regarding trinitarianism and the Gospel of John came from an atheist theology major in the class. This same person was the *only* student who actively reached out to see if I was safe in the aftermath of the campus shooting mentioned above. Put simply, this student contributed to my intellectual and spiritual formation as a Christian, but I could have dismissed these contributions because the student was an atheist. If I had done so, I would have missed a way that God was working to shape me.

performs the sacred text repeatedly over an extended period of time and in a disciplined, intentional way to gain a deeper understanding of God. Our use of "practice" is typological, pointing to an orderly process of human formation that assumes one's skill is not inherited at birth as a natural endowment that requires little work. Likewise, it assumes that one's repeated practice of a particular skill is not an aimless endeavor in which practice is the end in itself but rather a carefully selected means that targets human formation. Just as people practice certain skills, drills, and exercises so that they can become capable and well-performing musicians and athletes, the same holds true, we argue, for capable and well-performing biblical interpreters.[7]

"Practices," as we use the term, are fully wakeful routines intended to form a faithful congregation that purposes to mature into Christlikeness. Plenty could be said about this notion of practices, most of which is obvious when we think of the examples of athletes and musicians. First, practices take time. They cannot be undertaken in a rushed way to good effect, despite our culture's general impatience with taking the "long view" of things. Second, a practice requires intent: it cannot simply happen but must be chosen. A decision has to be made to pursue a practice. Third, practices are undertaken in community, despite our society's idolization of the individual. We need others for growth, support, and the expansion of our horizons. Finally, practices are goal-oriented. They are sought for particular purposes; they aim at something.

In sum, if a faithful congregation purposes to mature into Christlikeness, it needs (1) a vision of what Christlikeness looks like, (2) a holy, Spirit-inspired desire to pursue that vision, and (3) time to learn and develop (4) as a community. There is a logical relationship, then, between a congregation's performative practices and the holy ends to which God calls God's people. What is repeatedly practiced in worship and catechesis should always target the full salvation of a congregation's membership.

7. Here readers may see a connection with the Aristotelian-MacIntyrean account of practice, as found in Alasdair MacIntyre, *After Virtue*. Although there are certainly connections, we do not want to restrict ourselves definitionally to this account, given how extensive, intricate, and ultimately nontheological it is. We see a complementary vision to ours in Dykstra and Bass, "Theological Understanding of Christian Practices."

This typology of practice requires elaboration and application in light of our theological account of Scripture since it is fundamental to that account. For starters, we are claiming that there is such a thing as the *practice* of Scripture. The ontology and teleology of Scripture cannot simply be talked about in isolated settings; rather, these need to be on display in a congregation's practices, in its worship and confession. One might even say that within our preferred church-Scripture analogy, there is a liveliness within the very "hyphen" itself: it represents a kind of vibrancy that cannot simply be communicated textually. With this limit acknowledged, however, we will venture some remarks, given the nature of the present medium.

A most basic claim to be made here is that the Bible has to be actively read and heeded over time so that it resonates with the worshiping faithful *as* Sacred Scripture. Believers must want to know and to order their lives according to Scripture; its authority for life is something that is caught, not taught. Such usage is highlighted in Scripture itself. For example, according to our reading, the claim in 2 Peter that the Spirit enables the Old Testament prophets (and by implication the New Testament apostles) to speak on God's behalf (2 Pet. 1:20–21) would be untenable if it were only concerned with a certain take on the phenomenology of prophetic speech—heard once by its first witnesses but then never again remembered or heard from in new contexts. In fact, the enduring authority of 2 Peter is underwritten by the claim of apostolic authority precisely because the memories of the apostles continue to be recalled and reclaimed as God's word for new audiences of God's people.[8] A precanonical collection of Pauline letters is even mentioned as a scriptural source of spiritual wisdom (2 Pet. 3:15), similarly, we presume, to the Pauline testimony in 2 Timothy of Israel's scripture, whose performances are divinely inspired and therefore useful in forming the spiritually wise and morally mature. Our point is as evident as it is important: The Holy Spirit did not guide the church's postbiblical reception and recognition of those texts it had sanctified for holy ends without also intending the church catholic to perform them—to read and to heed them—so as to form a holy people belonging to God.

8. In particular see Nienhuis and Wall, *Reading the Epistles*, esp. 255–56.

Moreover, a faithful congregation's practice of Scripture is never an autonomous or independent activity. As with every other covenant-keeping activity, faithful readers practice the church's Scripture in community with other saints under the aegis of God's Spirit, who baptizes the Bible's various performances in worship, instruction, mission, and devotions into God's salvation-creating grace. Contrary to the approaches of modern criticism, which tend to valorize the attentive Bible student who hotly pursues a text's single normative meaning, we think Scripture's ongoing interpretation looks more like the constructive conversation that requires its participants to listen well and interact humbly in order to learn important goods from one another. In this way, one's interpretive horizons can be expanded—one can come to see the text differently when one reads it in the company of others—and one's vision of God can be expanded as a result.

As a congregation fulfills a desire to read and heed Scripture together over time so as to grow into Christlikeness in the power of the Holy Spirit, it will grow in wisdom and maturity. Such is not simply a work of God or a work of human striving but rather the result of a covenant partnership sustained by fidelity and love. Out of a love for God, believers will attend to the means of grace God has granted them to sustain them in the vicissitudes and challenges of life. One such means, as we have argued, is Scripture. Out of faithfulness to God, a congregation will recognize Scripture as canon, as a diverse collection of literary compositions addressed to audiences in response to crises that emerged within their ancient social worlds. We affirm that these ordinary texts were sanctified by the Holy Spirit for the church's practice of them in forming saints who truly love God and all their neighbors.

The Academy and the Church

How does the practice of Scripture relate to the academic guild of biblical studies? What role, if any, does formal investigation into the biblical world and texts have for a worshiping congregation intent on "practicing Scripture"? After all, one could argue, as Stephen Fowl has, that "reading Scripture theologically is first and foremost a practice of the church. It does not depend on the support of academics for its survival." One could take such remarks as inviting a certain kind of ignorance and neglect with regard to the achievements of formal biblical scholarship. In this vein, one may or may not appeal to such work, depending on the exigency of the moment (what will help make the desired point) or the trustworthiness of the source (whether a particular author or publisher is deemed "safe"). But consider what Fowl further states: "Nevertheless, disciplined, scholarly attention to interpreting Scripture theologically can only benefit the practice within the church."[9] Likely many within the church are not compelled by what Fowl deems as self-evident.

Why is this so? The failure of instruction, both ecclesial and academic, that would otherwise clarify the ontology and teleology of Scripture, too often results in an inability to engage the effective results of biblical scholarship with both discernment and appreciation. In absence of a practical theology of Scripture, conservative readers tend to disregard modern criticism's close reading of Scripture as somehow subversive in forming a robust faith. Furthermore, the regnant paradigm of meaning making (religious, cultural, or otherwise) generally fills the void left behind. It is our belief that many who strive after the meaning of biblical texts in an exclusively historical mode (that is, the normative meaning of a biblical text rests solely on what its author intended to communicate to the first audience in their ancient social setting) do so because the historian's gaze is the paradigm of choice for securing meaning in light of no other hermeneutical, epistemological, or theological alternative.

Therefore, in our attempt to secure the authority of Scripture by means of highlighting its ontology and teleology, we hope to create space for what some may deem to be threatening claims—but they are claims that we find necessary to affirm throughout. Our first affirmation acknowledges the material nature of biblical texts. As such, the Bible is first studied as a library of literary compositions, which surely includes careful linguistic analysis of texts and rigorous learning of the religious and social worlds that originally shaped their authors' communicative intentions. Modern biblical criticism has helped the church enormously in developing a range of

---

9. Fowl, *Theological Interpretation of Scripture*, 23.

exegetical practices that have enabled readers to learn the plain sense of biblical texts.[10] To be clear, we contend that what should motivate such care is not the recovery of a text's normative meaning by reconstructing its real author and then imagining what his communicative intent was for his first readers (or hearers). Nor is our ambition to reconstruct the ancient historical referent behind the text or even to analyze its literary properties as though such activities will move us closer to a single, normative meaning. While accepting biblical texts as authored compositions shaped by the historical contingencies and literary conventions of antiquity, we contend that their postbiblical appointment by the Spirit as an auxiliary of its continuing role in teaching disciples about the risen One reshapes how we understand Scripture's historical and literary properties and so also the aims of historical and literary criticisms.

We do acknowledge that the Bible's own idea of the real world is profoundly theological. It provides the context in which people witness and experience God at work in accomplishing God's redemptive plan through Jesus. Scripture's two-Testament narrative of this history has as its true referent not the narrated events per se but its witness to a God whose activities in history make all things new. This theological conception of history changes how we understand the aims of historical approaches to Scripture. We seek neither to remove God from history nor to remove history from God but to learn more about God within the movement of history as Scripture narrates it. Our practice of historical investigation does not pretend to keep theological commitments at arm's length but brings those very commitments to Scripture's own description of God's work in history.

At the same time, a literary approach to Scripture presumes that our reception of its witness to God is framed by the various genres and idioms of Scripture's witness to God's saving activity in history.[11] That is, the faithful reader of biblical texts is alert not only to the literary conventions practiced at the time of composition but also to how these conventions are employed to communicate a meaningful

---

10. For a fluent treatment of this modern understanding of a text's "plain sense," see Barton, *Nature of Biblical Criticism*, 69–116.

11. See Gaventa, "Toward a Theology of Acts," 146–57.

word from God to God's people. Faithfulness and scholarly engagement need not be at cross-purposes; on the contrary, we believe each requires the other.

A Curriculum for Reading the Church's Scripture

What we have offered is a broad account of the constitutive features of what can be termed "the practice of Scripture" and of how this practice envisions a congregation relying on (rather than neglecting) the work of biblical scholarship. In educational settings, visions such as these require an ordered account, a course of study—in short, a curriculum—listing their various aspects and laying the groundwork for their possible enactment. Faithful Bible study is in part an intuitive exercise that depends on the intellectual and spiritual maturity of the reader. As such, the breadth of one's learning and personal experiences is an indispensable element in the reader's schooling. But Bible study is also an intellectual and spiritual discipline that may be seen as a process of learning ordered by a curriculum of interdependent exercises. Each is an exercise of theological exegesis: the careful investigation of biblical texts that seeks a word from God for the people of God.

What follows, then, is our proposal for such a curriculum, whether for a university or seminary's classroom or for interested laypeople in service of their congregation. The proposal is meant to be a blueprint or road map to the "practice of Scripture" (as we have discussed it in this chapter), and it will offer a number of subpractices or exercises that aim to contribute to the overall goals we have highlighted in this chapter and throughout this book.

The Theological Ends of Critical Exegesis

We consider exegesis to be a way of doing theology. By this we mean that the reader's search for meaning resists the modern inclination to divide the tasks of exegesis from a thoughtful reflection on the exegeted text's distinctive witness to God. As we have said, for us they are of a piece. Nonetheless, in our work with the biblical text we must first of all become intimately acquainted with what it says.

The initial endeavoring of exegesis is translation. For most students, this is done by others who produce the modern translations the church uses in worship and instruction. We suggest that students (and also busy clergy) compare several translations of the exegeted text, including the one favored by their own worshiping community. Differing translations of the same passage sometimes expose the polyvalence of the Hebrew and Greek originals and thereby identify points of potential disagreement between different readers. When the polyvalence is especially strong, further study of such passages may be required.

Scripture's witness to God comes to us forged within ancient social and religious worlds. To hear the chorus of Scripture's witnesses requires us to learn something of the worlds wrapped around the biblical texts appointed by the Spirit for our theological understanding. Any exegetical practice that interrogates these texts within these ancient worlds may help the reader better understand in what ways each presents a discrete witness to God. But even if we pay attention to the scholarly consensus of this historical and linguistic work, this work is engaged with intellectual humility, recognizing that a "scholarly consensus" is always provisional and contested.

Exegesis that serves a community's theological understanding is careful to focus on the text's portrait of God and God's work in history. Careful exegesis is never the mere interrogation of a text for information *about* its author, its literary genre and social world, its linguistic style and rhetorical design, and so on. The results of this kind of interrogation, while illuminating, do not extend the holy ends of Scripture, which are formative of a faithful congregation's theological understanding. Moreover, the distance created by concentrating on the text's "original" sense may preempt its potential meaning for subsequent readers; such work may establish what the text "meant in the past" but be less adept in elaborating what it "means today."

This gap may be bridged if the scholar's interests are reoriented intellectually—if only by an act of hermeneutical repentance—so as to translate scholarly readings in a way that enables today's congregations to encounter the living God, but in a more informed way than is possible through devotional readings. That is, those humanistic virtues cultivated by the modern academy (such as a reader's

self-criticism and rigorous linguistic analysis of the text) may complement a reading regulated by a reader's theological commitments if
the endgame is theological (rather than cultural or historical) understanding. By analogy, the complementarity of these approaches,
critical and theological, is roughly similar to the complementary
relationship between the exemplary Paul of Acts and the frail Paul
who addresses us in 2 Corinthians. The point is this: The mutually
inclusive use of different reading strategies can result in a more fully
wakeful and attentive hearing of God's word in Scripture if under
the direction of God's Spirit.

The exercise of theologically critical exegesis also relies on another aspect we stress here. Our own theological commitments cue
a shift from a biblical text's compositional origins (and so its plain
sense at the intersection of the author's communicative intentions
for the first readers and their social and religious worlds) to the
text's postbiblical canonization and usage.[12] This includes a survey of the long history of the text's reception, application, and
effects within the church, which typically opens a window with
a better sight line into the full meaning of a biblical text and the
time-conditioned and conversational nature of its practice. Thus
theologically critical exegesis, as we see it, is both synchronic (committed to careful text-centered analysis) and diachronic (committed
to tracking the text's ongoing reception and variegated uses within
the church).

The Intertextuality of Two-Testament Exegesis

The final shape of Scripture envisions a pattern for reading it.
While this extends to the working relationships between the different parts of the whole (e.g., between the four Gospels or between
the Pentateuch and the Prophets), we have in mind especially the
relationship between the Old and New Testament witnesses to the
triune God and God's plan to restore all creation. A Bible curriculum
that explores the full potential of their intracanonical relationship

---

12. For an initial and provisional effort in comparing a biblical author's communicative intentions for writing his composition and the church's intentions for receiving
and reading the same text as Scripture, see Wall, "Acts of the Apostles," 5–11, 26–28.

will give students and parishioners honesty to encounter the dynamic interplay between these two witnesses and explore both their complementary continuity and their unsettling discontinuity.[13]

The curricular cue, of course, is the hermeneutics of Jesus, who commissioned his apostles to read Israel's scripture (i.e., the Old Testament) with the Holy Spirit to illumine its witness of his messianic life. Whether Israel's "partial hardening" toward Jesus (see Rom. 11:25) or the church's supersessionist hardening toward Israel is as much a moral failure as a hermeneutical one, the continuing conversation between Scripture's two Testaments presumes that both are sanctified witnesses to the one God who is incarnate in the one Messiah. The New Testament's allusions to and quotations of the Old Testament underwrite this point: what becomes clear in Jesus has already been disclosed in the Old Testament's "many parts" and these "in many ways" (Πολυμερῶς καὶ πολυτρόπως, polymerōs kai polytropos, Heb. 1:1). Reading the Old Testament gospels of the prophets, each being a discrete witness to God, is the necessary preparation for a theological reading of the New Testament gospels of the apostles, which is more easily recognized by rereading the Old Testament after a close reading of the New.[14]

The interpretive relationship between the two Testaments, whether investigated as a historical or a theological matter, is profoundly complex. We contend that only its persistent execution forms the interpretive skill—indeed the theological intuition—needed to effectively moderate the sometimes difficult conversation between the two Testaments and by extension between the one holy prophetic Israel and the one holy apostolic church. We recommend the use of a lectionary in forming an interpreter's awareness and the skills required to enter into this conversation. Whether ancient or modern, preformed or individually constructed, we suggest only that its format follow the traditional order of lessons: Old Testament, Psalter, New Testament, and Gospel.

There are three reasons for our recommendation to use a lectionary. First, a lectionary orders the reading of Scripture in a way that

---

13. Barr, *Concept of Biblical Theology*, 172–208.
14. See Wall, "Intertextuality, Biblical."

naturally facilitates a conversation between the two Testaments and so exposes their intertextuality. Quite apart from the intentions of their authors and editors, careful exegesis of the prescribed lessons exposes the linguistic and thematic links that relate them together in imaginatively new ways. The scope of the selected lessons typically covers the scope of Scripture, thereby exposing readers to a range of biblical witnesses that they might otherwise neglect.

Second, a lectionary's public reading and exposition, whether in a congregation or classroom, focuses its audience on Scripture. For those whose theology of Scripture affirms its role as God's word for God's people, this movement of Scripture outward to its hearers cultivates the indispensable dispositions for its Spirit-illumined reception as good news: attentive listening, honest self-criticism, new (and often unsettling) ways of learning God, and so on.

Finally, the sequence or movement of a lectionary's appointed lessons instantiates the hermeneutics of Jesus: from Israel's scripture (Old Testament, Psalms) to the apostolic eyewitness (New Testament) of the risen Jesus (Gospel). Moreover, the movement of the church's traditional lectionary targets its liturgical calendar, whose annual seasons follow the Gospel's narrative of Jesus's messianic mission to save the world. While we encourage a close reading of each lesson in its own context (historical, compositional, canonical) as a discrete, distinctive witness to God, the movement of lessons and its ecclesial target cultivate a keen awareness of Jesus's demand that his disciples learn to read the various collections of Scripture as an integral witness to himself and his redemptive mission.

Today's use of social media enhances all the more the use of a lectionary to practice and participate in Scripture's intracanonical conversation between its two Testaments. If a common lectionary (e.g., the Revised Common Lectionary) is practiced, the interpreter is assured that others around the world will be working on the same lessons Sunday by Sunday. Teachers and clergy may be encouraged to build networks with others for the purpose of sharing insights. Conversations should include multiple texts and the different communities each text represents, but also other saints from the global church who are shaped by different cultures and experiences that enable them to hear bits of God's word that others may not.

The Rule of Faithful Exegesis

Biblical texts do not carry a single normative meaning that moves easily between different social settings and time zones. While modern criticism actively seeks the text's putative author(s) in order to explain and establish its normative meaning, postmodern criticism turns its focus from the authors' communicative intentions for their first readers to its contemporary readers and the cultural forces and interests that have shaped them as decisive in meaning making. "Texts don't mean; people mean with texts."[15] As such, self-criticism is a more important attribute than historical or literary criticisms in regulating the interpretive act.

What is absent from the above synthesis of contemporary interpretive options is the overarching concern of faithful readers to protect the text from self-interested interpretations that reduce a text's multivalent meaning to just one in order to help secure and privilege a particular ideology or theology. Often lacking is an honest analysis of the text's plain sense controlled by modern criticisms of one kind or another rather than a community's ideational or theological interests.

Nonetheless, sin still happens. In part because of the inherent elasticity of textual meaning, the reader's analysis of any text can be manipulated to serve selfish ends. The practical problem that modern biblical criticism seeks to solve remains. While we welcome the use of a full array of modern criticisms to accomplish this task and to protect biblical texts from interpretive misuse, we have argued in this book that biblical interpretation still must be regulated to safeguard Scripture's apostolic deposit and its intended ends: to form a covenant-keeping community whose love for God and for neighbor is brought to maturity through worship and catechesis, mission, and personal devotions.

Even though Scripture's legal address is the church, the principal controls imposed by contemporary linguistic analysis pay relatively little attention to the spiritual effects of an interpreted text. For this reason, we propose the use of an apostolic Rule of Faith, which constrains what an interpreter may or may not retrieve from a biblical text for

15. Martin, *Pedagogy of the Bible*, 30.

theological instruction.[16] This regulatory norm is not a substitute for but a complement to the standard rules of modern biblical criticism.

Our advocacy of a theological rule is predicated on its use during canonization to regulate the reception and shaping of Scripture's final form. The early church's attentiveness to the content and grammar of the apostles' core beliefs cued not only its postbiblical recognition of which texts should be included in the New Testament canon but also what beliefs should be retrieved from their interpretation and use. On the basis of this circularity, the continuing use of this apostolic Rule of Faith should not only regulate the critical retrieval of theological goods from the sacred text; it should also supply an apt grammar of theological agreements that arranges those goods into a coherent articulation of God's word in worship and instruction, mission, and personal devotions.

Robert Jenson argues that this "*regula fidei* was a communal linguistic awareness of the faith delivered to the apostles" and was no text at all.[17] Although we are not satisfied with his fuller discussion of this point, it may help explain why the use of this metric to interpret and use biblical texts is more intuitive than a formal intellectual exercise. In Jenson's mind, the Rule of Faith is "adduced," since its various expressions in the ancient church imply that this apostolic deposit was never reduced to a single normative form.

One of the best examples of this apostolic Rule in our mind is the one that functioned as the principal theological constraint during the formation of the biblical canon, as found in Tertullian's *Prescription against Heretics*. The great Apologist set out the following core beliefs of a theological grammar whose application helped a postbiblical church discern between apostolic and nonapostolic articulations of God's word, work that in turn helped form the essential theological understanding of a truly catholic church:

1. **The Creator God**: "There is only one God, and . . . He is none other than the Creator of the world, who produced all things out of nothing through His own Word, first of all sent forth."

---

16. For an introduction to the use of an ancient version of the apostolic Rule of Faith to guide the exegesis of a biblical text, see Wall, *1 & 2 Timothy and Titus*, 40–43.

17. Jenson, *Canon and Creed*, 14–18.

2. **Christ Jesus the Lord**: "This Word is called His Son, and, under the name of God, was seen 'in diverse manners' by the patriarchs, heard at all times in the prophets, at last brought down by the Spirit and Power of the Father into the Virgin Mary, was made flesh in her womb, and, being born of her, went forth as Jesus Christ; thenceforth He preached the new law and the new promise of the kingdom of heaven, worked miracles; having been crucified, He rose again the third day; (then) having ascended into the heavens, He sat at the right hand of the Father."

3. **Community of the Spirit**: "Christ sent instead of Himself the Power of the Holy Ghost to lead such as believe."[18]

4. **Christian Existence/Discipleship**: "For in putting on our flesh, Christ made it his own; and in making it his own, he made it sinless . . . because in that same human flesh he lived without sin."[19]

5. **Consummation in a New Creation**: "Christ will come with glory to take the saints to the enjoyment of everlasting life and of the heavenly promises, and to condemn the wicked to everlasting fire, after the resurrection of both these classes shall have happened, together with the restoration of their flesh."[20]

Whether this or another framework is used, faithful readers of Scripture will be ruled by the Rule of Faith in terms of both where they come from and where they land as the Bible is read and performed in contexts of worship and formation. The Rule functions as a "standard of excellence" for determining virtuosity, skill, and exquisiteness in the practice of Scripture.

18. The creed's idiom of a "catholic church" is not used. Rather, the sense in Tertullian's writings is more local and congregational in force. This follows Paul, whose ecclesiology hardly ever prescribes belief in a "catholic" church (although perhaps so in Ephesians). Clearly in the Pastoral Epistles, as elsewhere in the Pauline canon, the focus is on a local congregation of believers and on individuals or individual subgroups within it. For this reason, the use of "community" rather than "church" may be preferable when articulating points of these theological agreements.

19. This remark is from Tertullian, *On the Flesh of Christ* 16.

20. Tertullian, *Prescription against Heretics* 13.

The Adaptation of Scripture to Contemporary Life

The final task of a wise and mature practice of Scripture is to contemporize the message of a biblical text to underscore its practical relevance for its current readers. Jewish Bible scholar Daniel Boyarin calls this practice "comparative midrash."[21] Midrash is a rabbinical term (from the Hebrew verb *dārash*) for biblical commentary engaging in a disciplined, imaginative search for meaning that establishes theological continuity between the past of God's word as witnessed in Scripture and the present moment when new questions and crises challenge faithful readers to seek a fresh understanding of God's word in Scripture. Often this includes finding creative solutions to textual contradictions or clarifying the relevance of obscure meanings that might otherwise compromise the authority of a biblical text. Boyarin perceives the biblical text as "gapped" and sees the role of the interpretive community as entering into a dialogue with the text in order to complete it by filling in its gaps in culturally relevant ways. While there are evident dangers with his approach, what Boyarin emphasizes is important: the conversation the church enters into with its Scripture must include the symbols, controversies, forces, and factors of the contemporary world in which we live. If the question "What?" concentrates the exegetical task, the question "So what?" concentrates readers on the target of the holy word we retrieve from the text.

We have sometimes characterized the practical value of Scripture's own diversity as establishing an apparatus of checks and balances. On the one hand, this diversity is fixed by the canon itself: it cannot include a witness to God that is not found within Scripture. Scripture's full witness to God's gospel is a whole that at the very least is a sum of its parts. Whenever Scripture is used to form a community's theological understanding, every part of this whole must be consulted. On the other hand, no one part of this whole canon has veto power over any other part. The interpretive practice of resisting any canon within the canon makes it impossible to use that canon as a blunt instrument to harmonize all other canonical witnesses in agreement with itself. The New Testament must be read with the Old Testament,

---

21. See Boyarin, *Intertextuality and the Reading of Midrash*, 1–21.

the Synoptic Gospels with the Fourth Gospel, and the Pauline Letters with the Catholic Letters—and the book of Revelation must not be left out of our Sunday readings!

Finally, in this day when an appeal to sociology is often elevated over theology as the end of biblical interpretation, we remain steadfast in our theology of Scripture as God's word for God's people. Congregations and classrooms must be taught that reading Scripture does not serve sociological ends; it is not a weapon in any cultural war or philosophical disputation. The practical role of Scripture is to provide the Holy Spirit with a sanctified auxiliary by which to form a holy people who know and love God with all their hearts and minds. In this, the marks of the church and the marks of Scripture go hand in hand.

Bibliography

Abraham, William J. *Canon and Criterion in Christian Theology: From the Fathers to Feminism*. Oxford: Oxford University Press, 1998.

Abraham, William J., Jason E. Vickers, and Natalie B. Van Kirk, eds. *Canonical Theism: A Proposal for Theology and the Church*. Grand Rapids: Eerdmans, 2008.

Adam, A. K. M. "Docetism, Käsemann, and Christology." *Scottish Journal of Theology* 49 (1996): 391–410.

Athanasius. *Letters to Serapion*. In Athanasius the Great and Didymus the Blind, *Works on the Spirit*, translated by Mark DelCogliano, Andrew Radde-Gallwitz, and Lewis Ayres, 53–137. Yonkers, NY: St. Vladimir's Seminary Press, 2011.

———. *On the Incarnation*. Translated by a Religious of C. S. M. V. Crestwood, NY: St. Vladimir's Seminary Press, 2002.

Ayres, Lewis, and Stephen E. Fowl. "(Mis)Reading the Face of God." *Theological Studies* 60 (1999): 513–28.

Barr, James. *The Concept of Biblical Theology: An Old Testament Perspective*. Minneapolis: Fortress, 1999.

Barth, Karl. *Church Dogmatics*. 4 vols. Edited by Geoffrey W. Bromiley and Thomas F. Torrance. Edinburgh: T&T Clark, 1956–75.

Barth, Markus. *Conversation with the Bible*. New York: Holt, Rinehart and Winston, 1964.

Barton, John. *The Nature of Biblical Criticism*. Louisville: Westminster John Knox, 2007.

Bauckham, Richard. "James and the Gentiles (Acts 15:13–21)." In *History, Literature, and Society in the Book of Acts*, edited by Ben Witherington, 154–84. Cambridge: Cambridge University Press, 1996.

Beale, G. K. *A New Testament Biblical Theology: The Unfolding of the Old Testament in the New*. Grand Rapids: Baker Academic, 2011.

Billings, J. Todd. *The Word of God for the People of God: An Entryway to the Theological Interpretation of Scripture*. Grand Rapids: Eerdmans, 2010.

Bovon, François. *Luke*. 3 vols. Minneapolis: Fortress, 2012–13.

Boyarin, Daniel. *Intertextuality and the Reading of Midrash*. Bloomington: Indiana University Press, 1994.

Boyer, Steven D., and Christopher A. Hall. *The Mystery of God: Theology for Knowing the Unknowable*. Grand Rapids: Baker Academic, 2012.

Brueggemann, Walter. *The Bible Makes Sense*. Louisville: Westminster John Knox, 1977.

Calvin, John. *Institutes of the Christian Religion*. Vol. 1. Edited by John T. McNeill. Philadelphia: Westminster, 1960.

Campbell, Ted. "Negotiating Wesleyan Catholicity." In *Embodying Wesley's Catholic Spirit*, edited by Daniel Castelo, 1–17. Eugene, OR: Pickwick, 2017.

Castelo, Daniel. "Inspiration as Providence." In *The Usefulness of Scripture: Essays in Honor of Robert W. Wall*, edited by Daniel Castelo, Sara M. Koenig, and David R. Nienhuis, 69–81. University Park, PA: Eisenbrauns, 2018.

———. *Pneumatology: A Guide for the Perplexed*. London: T&T Clark, 2015.

———. "The Spirit, Creaturehood and Sanctification: On Avoiding Theological Overcompensation." *International Journal of Systematic Theology* 16 (2014): 177–91.

Castelo, Daniel, and Robert W. Wall. "Scripture and the Church: A Précis for an Alternative Analogy." *Journal of Theological Interpretation* 5, no. 2 (2011): 197–210.

Catechism of the Catholic Church. New York: Image Doubleday, 1995.

Childs, Brevard S. *The Church's Guide for Reading Paul: The Canonical Shaping of the Pauline Corpus*. Grand Rapids: Eerdmans, 2008.

Cleveland, Christena. *Disunity in Christ: Uncovering the Hidden Forces That Keep Us Apart*. Downers Grove, IL: InterVarsity, 2013.

Dykstra, Craig, and Dorothy C. Bass. "A Theological Understanding of Christian Practices." In *Practicing Theology: Beliefs and Practices in*

Christian Life, edited by Miroslav Volf and Dorothy C. Bass, 13–32. Grand Rapids: Eerdmans, 2002.

Enns, Peter. *Inspiration and Incarnation: Evangelicals and the Problem of the Old Testament*. 2nd ed. Grand Rapids: Baker Academic, 2015.

Flett, John G. *Apostolicity: The Ecumenical Question in World Christian Perspective*. Downers Grove, IL: IVP Academic, 2016.

Fowl, Stephen E. *Theological Interpretation of Scripture*. Eugene, OR: Cascade, 2009.

———. "Virtue." In *Dictionary for Theological Interpretation of the Bible*, edited by Kevin Vanhoozer, 837–39. Grand Rapids: Baker Academic, 2005.

Gaventa, Beverly R. "Toward a Theology of Acts: Reading and Rereading." *Interpretation* 42 (1988): 146–57.

Gorman, Michael. *Elements of Biblical Exegesis: A Basic Guide for Students and Ministers*. Rev. ed. Peabody, MA: Hendrickson, 2009.

Goroncy, Jason. "The Elusiveness, Loss and Cruciality of Recovered Holiness." *International Journal of Systematic Theology* 10 (2008): 195–209.

Green, Joel B. *The Gospel of Luke*. New International Commentary on the New Testament. Grand Rapids: Eerdmans, 1997.

Gregory of Nazianzus. *Epistle 101*. In *Cyril of Jerusalem, Gregory Nazianzen*, vol. 7 of *Nicene and Post-Nicene Fathers*, 2nd series. Edited by Philip Schaff and Henry Wace. New York: Christian Literature Company, 1890. Reprint, Peabody, MA: Hendrickson, 1994.

Griffiths, Jonathan I. *Hebrews and Divine Speech*. Library of New Testament Studies 507. London: T&T Clark, 2014.

Gundry, Robert H. *Peter: False Disciple and Apostate according to Saint Matthew*. Grand Rapids: Eerdmans, 2015.

Harnack, Adolf von. *History of Dogma*. 7 vols. Boston: Little, Brown, 1895–1900.

Hauerwas, Stanley. "On Doctrine and Ethics." In *The Cambridge Companion to Christian Doctrine*, edited by Colin E. Gunton, 21–40. Cambridge: Cambridge University Press, 1997.

Hays, Richard B. *Echoes of Scripture in the Gospels*. Waco: Baylor University Press, 2016.

Hockey, Katherine M., Madison N. Pierce, and Francis Watson, eds. *Muted Voices of the New Testament: Readings in the Catholic Epistles and Hebrews*. New York: T&T Clark, 2017.

Hodge, Charles. *Systematic Theology*. 3 vols. 1871. Reprint, Peabody, MA: Hendrickson, 2003.

Jenson, Robert W. *Canon and Creed*. Louisville: Westminster John Knox, 2010.

Johnson, Luke T. *The Letter of James*. New Haven: Yale University Press, 1995.

Käsemann, Ernst. "Vom theologischen Recht historisch-kritischer Exegese." *Zeitschrift für Theologie und Kirche* 64, no. 3 (1967): 259–81.

Kilby, Karen. "Perichoresis and Projection: Problems with Social Doctrines of the Trinity." *New Blackfriars* 81, no. 957 (2000): 432–45.

Kinnaman, David. *You Lost Me: Why Young Christians Are Leaving Church and Rethinking Faith*. Grand Rapids: Baker Books, 2011.

Knight, Henry H., III. *The Presence of God in the Christian Life: John Wesley and the Means of Grace*. Metuchen, NJ: Scarecrow, 1992.

Legaspi, Michael. *The Death of Scripture and the Rise of Biblical Studies*. Oxford: Oxford University Press, 2010.

Leithart, Peter J. *Defending Constantine: The Twilight of an Empire and the Dawn of Christendom*. Downers Grove, IL: InterVarsity, 2010.

Lemcio, Eugene E. *The Past of Jesus in the Gospels*. Society for New Testament Studies Monograph Series 68. Cambridge: Cambridge University Press, 2005.

———. "The Unifying Kerygma of the New Testament." *Journal for the Study of the New Testament* 33 (1988): 3–17.

———. "The Unifying Kerygma of the New Testament (II)." *Journal for the Study of the New Testament* 38 (1990): 3–11.

Levenson, Jon D. "The Eighth Principle of Judaism and the Literary Simultaneity of Scripture." *Journal of Religion* 68 (1988): 205–25.

Lim, Bo H., and Daniel Castelo. *Hosea*. Grand Rapids: Eerdmans, 2015.

MacIntyre, Alasdair. *After Virtue*. 3rd ed. Notre Dame, IN: University of Notre Dame Press, 2007.

Martin, Dale B. *Pedagogy of the Bible: An Analysis and Proposal*. Louisville: Westminster John Knox, 2008.

Moberly, R. W. L. "'Interpret the Bible like Any Other Book'?" *Journal of Theological Interpretation* 4 (2010): 91–110.

Nichols, Aidan. *The Shape of Catholic Theology: An Introduction to Its Sources, Principles, and History*. Collegeville, MN: Liturgical Press, 1991.

Nienhuis, David R., and Robert W. Wall. *Reading the Epistles of James, Peter, John, and Jude as Scripture*. Grand Rapids: Eerdmans, 2013.

Pardue, Stephen T. *The Mind of Christ: Humility and the Intellect in Early Christian Theology*. London: Bloomsbury T&T Clark, 2013.

Pew Research Center. "Global Christianity—A Report on the Size and Distribution of the World's Christian Population." December 19, 2011. www .pewforum.org/2011/12/19/global-christianity-exec.

Pontifical Biblical Commission. "Document on the Interpretation of the Bible in the Church." In *The Scripture Documents: An Anthology of Official Catholic Teaching*, edited by Dean P. Béchard, 244–317. Collegeville, MN: Liturgical Press, 2002.

Radner, Ephraim. *A Brutal Unity: The Spiritual Politics of the Christian Church*. Waco: Baylor University Press, 2012.

Schlabach, Gerald W. *Unlearning Protestantism: Sustaining Christian Community in an Unstable Age*. Grand Rapids: Brazos, 2010.

Seitz, Christopher. *Word Without End: The Old Testament as Abiding Theological Witness*. Waco: Baylor University Press, 2005.

Spina, Frank A. "Israel as a Figure for the Church." In *The Usefulness of Scripture: Essays in Honor of Robert W. Wall*, edited by Daniel Castelo, Sara M. Koenig, and David R. Nienhuis, 3–23. University Park, PA: Eisenbrauns, 2018.

Strawn, Brent. "Docetism, Käsemann, and Christology." *Journal of Theological Interpretation* 2 (2008): 161–80.

Talbert, Charles H. *Reading Acts: A Literary and Theological Commentary*. Rev. ed. Macon, GA: Smyth & Helwys, 2013.

Tertullian. *On the Flesh of Christ*. In *Latin Christianity: Its Founder, Tertullian*, vol. 3 of *The Ante-Nicene Fathers: Translations of the Writings of the Fathers down to A.D. 325*. Edited by Alexander Roberts and James Donaldson. 10 vols. 1885–1887. Reprint, Peabody, MA: Hendrickson, 1994.

———. *Prescription against Heretics*. In *Latin Christianity: Its Founder, Tertullian*, vol. 3 of *The Ante-Nicene Fathers: Translations of the Writings of the Fathers down to A.D. 325*. Edited by Alexander Roberts and James Donaldson. 10 vols. 1885–1887. Reprint, Peabody, MA: Hendrickson, 1994.

Thomas, John Christopher. *Footwashing in John 13 and the Johannine Community*. Sheffield: JSOT Press, 1991.

———. "Footwashing within the Context of the Lord's Supper." In *The Lord's Supper*, edited by Dale R. Stoffer, 169–84. Scottdale, PA: Herald Press, 1997.

Tillich, Paul. *The Protestant Era*. Chicago: University of Chicago Press, 1948.

Torrance, Thomas F. *Incarnation: The Person and Life of Christ*. Edited by Robert T. Walker. Downers Grove, IL: IVP Academic, 2008.

Tracy, David. *The Analogical Imagination: Christian Theology and the Culture of Pluralism*. New York: Crossroad, 1981.

Turner, Denys. "Apophaticism, Idolatry, and the Claims of Reason." In *Silence and the Word: Negative Theology and Incarnation*, edited by Oliver Davies and Denys Turner, 11–34. Cambridge: Cambridge University Press, 2002.

Van De Walle, Bernie A. *Rethinking Holiness: A Theological Introduction*. Grand Rapids: Baker Academic, 2017.

Volf, Miroslav. "'The Trinity Is Our Social Program': The Doctrine of the Trinity and the Shape of Social Engagement." *Modern Theology* 14 (1998): 403–23.

Wall, Robert W. "The Acts of the Apostles." In *New Interpreter's Bible*, vol. 10, edited by Leander E. Keck, 1–368. Nashville: Abingdon, 2002.

———. "Canon." In *The Oxford Encyclopedia of the Bible and Theology*, vol. 1, edited by Samuel E. Balantine, 111–21. Oxford: Oxford University Press, 2015.

———. *1 & 2 Timothy and Titus*. Grand Rapids: Eerdmans, 2014.

———. "Intertextuality, Biblical." In *Dictionary of New Testament Background: A Compendium of Contemporary Biblical Scholarship*, edited by Craig A. Evans and Stanley E. Porter, 541–51. Downers Grove, IL: InterVarsity, 2000.

———. "Reading Paul with Acts: The Canonical Shaping of a Holy Church." In *Holiness and Ecclesiology in the New Testament*, edited by Kent E. Brower and Andy Johnson, 129–47. Grand Rapids: Eerdmans, 2007.

———. "The Rule of Faith in Theological Hermeneutics." In *Between Two Horizons: Spanning New Testament Studies and Systematic Theology*, edited by Joel B. Green and Max Turner, 88–107. Grand Rapids: Eerdmans, 1999.

Weber, Otto. *Foundations of Dogmatics*. Vol. 1. Grand Rapids: Eerdmans, 1981.

Webster, John. "Canon and Criterion: Some Reflections on a Recent Proposal." *Scottish Journal of Theology* 54 (2001): 221–37.

———. *Holy Scripture: A Dogmatic Sketch*. Cambridge: Cambridge University Press, 2003.

Wells, Samuel. *Improvisation: The Drama of Christian Ethics*. Grand Rapids: Brazos, 2004.

Wesley, John. "Journal Entry, 11 June 1739." In *The Bicentennial Edition of the Works of John Wesley*, vol. 19, edited by W. Reginald Ward and Richard P. Heitzenrater, 65–68. Nashville: Abingdon, 1990.

———. "The Means of Grace." In *The Bicentennial Edition of the Works of John Wesley*, vol. 1, edited by Albert C. Outler, 376–97. Nashville: Abingdon, 1984.

Westphal, Merold. *Whose Community? Which Interpretation? Philosophical Hermeneutics for the Church*. Grand Rapids: Baker Academic, 2009.

Wiarda, Timothy. *Spirit and Word: Dual Testimony in Paul, John and Luke*. London: Bloomsbury T&T Clark, 2017.

Work, Telford. *Living and Active: Scripture in the Economy of Salvation*. Grand Rapids: Eerdmans, 2002.

Scripture and Ancient Writings Index

170

Subject Index